Word 2010:
Intermediate
Student Manual

MOS Edition

Word 2010: Intermediate

Chief Executive Officer, Axzo Press:	Ken Wasnock
Series Designer and COO:	Adam A. Wilcox
Vice President, Operations:	Josh Pincus
Director of Publishing Systems Development:	Dan Quackenbush
Developmental Editor:	Chris Hale
Copyeditor:	Catherine Oliver
Keytester:	Cliff Coryea

Trademarks

ILT Series is a trademark of Axzo Press.

Some of the product names and company names used in this book have been used for identification purposes only and may be trademarks or registered trademarks of their respective manufacturers and sellers.

Disclaimer

We reserve the right to revise this publication and make changes from time to time in its content without notice.

Student Manual
ISBN 10: 1-4260-2165-8
ISBN 13: 978-1-4260-2165-7

Printed in the United States of America
1 2 3 4 5 GL 06 05 04 03

Contents

Introduction

After reading this introduction, you will know how to:

A Use ILT Series manuals in general.

B Use prerequisites, a target student description, course objectives, and a skills inventory to properly set your expectations for the course.

C Re-key this course after class.

Topic A: About the manual

ILT Series philosophy

Our manuals facilitate your learning by providing structured interaction with the software itself. While we provide text to explain difficult concepts, the hands-on activities are the focus of our courses. By paying close attention as your instructor leads you through these activities, you will learn the skills and concepts effectively.

We believe strongly in the instructor-led class. During class, focus on your instructor. Our manuals are designed and written to facilitate your interaction with your instructor, and not to call attention to manuals themselves.

We believe in the basic approach of setting expectations, delivering instruction, and providing summary and review afterwards. For this reason, lessons begin with objectives and end with summaries. We also provide overall course objectives and a course summary to provide both an introduction to and closure on the entire course.

Manual components

The manuals contain these major components:

- Table of contents
- Introduction
- Units
- Course summary
- Glossary
- Index

Each element is described below.

Table of contents

The table of contents acts as a learning roadmap.

Introduction

The introduction contains information about our training philosophy and our manual components, features, and conventions. It contains target student, prerequisite, objective, and setup information for the specific course.

Units

Units are the largest structural component of the course content. A unit begins with a title page that lists objectives for each major subdivision, or topic, within the unit. Within each topic, conceptual and explanatory information alternates with hands-on activities. Units conclude with a summary comprising one paragraph for each topic, and an independent practice activity that gives you an opportunity to practice the skills you've learned.

The conceptual information takes the form of text paragraphs, exhibits, lists, and tables. The activities are structured in two columns, one telling you what to do, the other providing explanations, descriptions, and graphics.

Course summary

This section provides a text summary of the entire course. It is useful for providing closure at the end of the course. The course summary also indicates the next course in this series, if there is one, and lists additional resources you might find useful as you continue to learn about the software.

Glossary

The glossary provides definitions for all of the key terms used in this course.

Index

The index at the end of this manual makes it easy for you to find information about a particular software component, feature, or concept.

Manual conventions

We've tried to keep the number of elements and the types of formatting to a minimum in the manuals. This aids in clarity and makes the manuals more classically elegant looking. But there are some conventions and icons you should know about.

Item	Description
Italic text	In conceptual text, indicates a new term or feature.
Bold text	In unit summaries, indicates a key term or concept. In an independent practice activity, indicates an explicit item that you select, choose, or type.
`Code font`	Indicates code or syntax.
`Longer strings of ▶` `    code will look ▶` `    like this.`	In the hands-on activities, any code that's too long to fit on a single line is divided into segments by one or more continuation characters (▶). This code should be entered as a continuous string of text.
Select **bold item**	In the left column of hands-on activities, bold sans-serif text indicates an explicit item that you select, choose, or type.
Keycaps like (↵ ENTER)	Indicate a key on the keyboard you must press.

Hands-on activities

The hands-on activities are the most important parts of our manuals. They are divided into two primary columns. The "Here's how" column gives short instructions to you about what to do. The "Here's why" column provides explanations, graphics, and clarifications. Here's a sample:

Do it!

A-1:   Creating a commission formula

Here's how	Here's why
1 Open Sales	This is an oversimplified sales compensation worksheet. It shows sales totals, commissions, and incentives for five sales reps.
2 Observe the contents of cell F4	F4 ▼ ◼ =E4*C_Rate The commission rate formulas use the name "C_Rate" instead of a value for the commission rate.

For these activities, we have provided a collection of data files designed to help you learn each skill in a real-world business context. As you work through the activities, you will modify and update these files. Of course, you might make a mistake and therefore want to re-key the activity starting from scratch. To make it easy to start over, you will rename each data file at the end of the first activity in which the file is modified. Our convention for renaming files is to add the word "My" to the beginning of the file name. In the above activity, for example, a file called "Sales" is being used for the first time. At the end of this activity, you would save the file as "My sales," thus leaving the "Sales" file unchanged. If you make a mistake, you can start over using the original "Sales" file.

In some activities, however, it might not be practical to rename the data file. If you want to retry one of these activities, ask your instructor for a fresh copy of the original data file.

Topic B: Setting your expectations

Properly setting your expectations is essential to your success. This topic will help you do that by providing:

- Prerequisites for this course
- A description of the target student
- A list of the objectives for the course
- A skills assessment for the course

Course prerequisites

Before taking this course, you should be familiar with personal computers and the use of a keyboard and a mouse. Furthermore, this course assumes that you've completed the following courses or have equivalent experience:

- *Windows 7: Basic*
- *Word 2010: Basic*

Target student

The target student for this course is an individual who wants to work more efficiently in Word 2010. You will work with styles, outlines, sections, and columns, format tables, print labels and envelopes, use templates and building blocks, work with graphics, manage document revisions, and use Web features.

MOS certification

This course is designed to help you pass the Microsoft Office Specialist (MOS) exam for Word 2010. For complete certification training, you should complete this course and all of the following:

- *Word 2010: Basic*
- *Word 2010: Advanced*

Course objectives

These overall course objectives will give you an idea about what to expect from the course. It is also possible that they will help you see that this course is not the right one for you. If you think you either lack the prerequisite knowledge or already know most of the subject matter to be covered, you should let your instructor know that you think you are misplaced in the class.

Note: In addition to the general objectives listed below, specific Microsoft Office Specialist exam objectives are listed at the beginning of each topic (where applicable).

After completing this course, you will know how to:

- Examine and compare text formatting of two selections; apply and create paragraph and character styles; modify, override, and export styles; and use Outline view and the Navigation pane to work with a document outline.

- Create and format sections of text by using section breaks, headers and footers, and page numbering; and format text into columns.

- Format tables, sort data in a table, and apply and modify table styles.

- Prepare and print labels and envelopes.

- Work with templates, use the Building Blocks Organizer, protect a document with a password, and view and edit document properties.

- Create and modify a diagram, insert and modify text boxes and shapes, and format text by using WordArt, drop caps, and pull quotes.

- Use Track Changes, review revisions, and work with comments.

- Preview and save a document as a Web page, and work with hyperlinks in a document.

Skills inventory

Use the following form to gauge your skill level entering the class. For each skill listed, rate your familiarity from 1 to 5, with five being the most familiar. *This is not a test.* Rather, it is intended to provide you with an idea of where you're starting from at the beginning of class. If you're wholly unfamiliar with all the skills, you might not be ready for the class. If you think you already understand all of the skills, you might need to move on to the next course in the series. In either case, you should let your instructor know as soon as possible.

Skill	1	2	3	4	5
Using the Reveal Formatting pane					
Applying styles					
Creating styles by example					
Basing one style on another					
Creating character styles					
Modifying styles					
Overriding a style					
Exporting styles					
Creating, organizing, and formatting outlines					
Inserting and deleting section breaks					
Formatting sections					
Inserting section headers and footers					
Formatting section page numbers					
Formatting text into columns and inserting column breaks					
Aligning text in table cells					
Merging and splitting table cells					
Changing row height					
Changing table borders and shading					
Sorting table data					
Splitting a table					
Repeating a table's header row					
Entering formulas in tables					

Skill	1	2	3	4	5
Applying and modifying table styles					
Printing labels and envelopes					
Using templates					
Using building blocks					
Protecting a document					
Viewing and editing document properties					
Creating and formatting organization charts					
Drawing and modifying shapes					
Inserting and formatting text boxes					
Arranging multiple objects					
Changing a shape into another shape					
Using WordArt					
Inserting and modifying drop caps					
Inserting pull quotes					
Tracking changes while editing					
Reviewing and accepting revisions					
Inserting and modifying comments					
Previewing and saving document as Web pages					
Inserting hyperlinks					

Topic C: Re-keying the course

If you have the proper hardware and software, you can re-key this course after class. This section explains what you'll need in order to do so, and how to do it.

Hardware requirements

Your personal computer should have:

- A keyboard and a mouse
- A 500 MHz (or faster) processor
- At least 256 MB of available RAM
- At least 1.5 GB of available hard drive space
- A monitor with at least 1024 × 768 resolution

Software requirements

You will also need the following software:

- Microsoft Windows 7 (You can also use Windows Vista or Windows XP, but the screenshots in this course were taken in Windows 7, so your screens might look somewhat different.)
- Microsoft Office 2010
- A printer driver (An actual printer is not required, but you will not be able to complete Activities A-1 or B-1 in the unit titled "Printing labels and envelopes" unless a driver is installed.)

Network requirements

The following network components and connectivity are also required for re-keying this course:

- Internet access, for the following purposes:
  - Downloading the latest critical updates and service packs
  - Completing Activity A-1 in the unit titled "Templates and building blocks"

Setup instructions to re-key the course

Before you re-key the course, you will need to perform the following steps:

1 Use Windows Update to install all available critical updates and service packs.
2 With flat-panel displays, we recommend using the panel's native resolution for best results. Color depth/quality should be set to High (24 bit) or higher.

   Note that your display settings or resolution might differ from the author's, so your screens might not exactly match the screen shots in this manual.

3   If necessary, reset any Word 2010 defaults that you have changed. If you do not wish to reset the defaults, you can still re-key the course, but some activities might not work exactly as documented.

    a   Delete the custom and downloaded templates from the Templates folder: C:\Users\\[*user name*]\AppData\Roaming\Microsoft\Templates. The AppData folder is hidden by default, but you can delete the templates from within Word. To do so:

        1   On the File tab, click New.

        2   Click My templates to open the New dialog box.

        3   Right-click and choose Delete to delete the templates. **Note:** Delete all templates *except* the Blank Document template.

        4   Click OK.

    b   Reset Track Changes settings to the defaults:

        1   On the Review tab, click Track Changes and choose Change Tracking Options.

        2   Next to Insertions, from the Color list, select By author.

        3   Next to Deletions, from the Color list, select By author.

        4   From the Use Balloons (Print and Web Layout) list, select "Only for comments/formatting." Click OK.

4   If you have the data disc that came with this manual, locate the Student Data folder on it and copy it to your Windows desktop.

If you don't have the data disc, you can download the Student Data files for the course:

    a   Connect to http://downloads.logicaloperations.com.

    b   Enter the course title or search by part to locate this course

    c   Click the course title to display a list of available downloads.
       Note: Data Files are located under the Instructor Edition of the course.

    d   Click the link(s) for downloading the Student Data files.

    e   Create a folder named Student Data on the desktop of your computer.

    f   Double-click the downloaded zip file(s) and drag the contents into the Student Data folder.

Unit 1

Styles and outlines

Unit time: 75 minutes

Complete this unit, and you'll know how to:

A Examine and compare text formatting by using the Reveal Formatting pane.

B Apply and create paragraph and character styles.

C Modify, override, and export styles.

D Create, organize, and format a document outline.

Topic A: Examining formatting

Explanation

You can tell what formatting you've applied to text by examining the Font and Paragraph dialog boxes or the Home tab. But a faster way to see the details of all of the formatting applied to a selection is to use the Reveal Formatting pane. In addition, you can use the Reveal Formatting pane to compare the formatting of two selections.

The Reveal Formatting pane

The Reveal Formatting pane displays the font and paragraph formatting of the selected text. To open the Reveal Formatting pane, press Shift+F1.

Select some text to view its formatting information. For example, in Exhibit 1-1, the heading "Contents" appears in the Selected text box. The applied formatting is displayed under "Formatting of selected text." Exhibit 1-1 shows that the heading is formatted as Trebuchet MS, 26 pt, bold, and that it has a custom color applied to it. You can click the blue underlined text to change the formatting.

Exhibit 1-1: The Reveal Formatting pane

Comparing formatting

You can use the Reveal Formatting pane to compare the text formatting of two selections. To do so, verify that the first selection appears in the Selected text box. Then, in the Reveal Formatting pane, check "Compare to another selection" to display a second Selected text box. Finally, in the document, select the text to be compared. The result of the comparison is shown in the Formatting differences box.

Do it!

A-1:   Using the Reveal Formatting pane

The files for this activity are in Student Data folder **Unit 1\Topic A**.

Here's how	Here's why
1 Start Word	
2 Open Cookbook1	
Save the document as **My cookbook1**	In the current topic folder.
3 Move to page 2	The Contents page.
4 Select the heading **Contents**	
5 Press (SHIFT) + (F1)	To open the Reveal Formatting pane, which displays the formatting of the selected text.
6 In the Reveal Formatting pane, click **Font**, as shown	**Formatting of selected text** ⊟ **Font** Font: (Default) Trebuchet MS 26 pt Bold To open the Font dialog box.
From the Size list, select **24**	
7 Click **Text Effects**	To open the Format Text Effects dialog box.
Click **Shadow**	
In the Presets gallery, select the indicated option	No Shadow A
Click **Close**	
8 Click **OK**	To close the Font dialog box. Word updates the Reveal Formatting pane to reflect the font and effect changes.
9 In the Reveal Formatting pane, check **Compare to another selection**	You'll compare the "Contents" heading with the heading on page 3.

10 Scroll to page 3

Select the heading **The long history of spices**

This heading's formatting is different from that of the other heading. You'll observe the differences in formatting and then set the formatting to match.

Observe the Formatting differences box

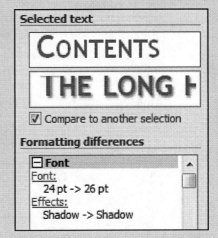

The differences between the two selections appear in the box. The first selection has a font size of 24 pt, while the second selection is 26 pt. In addition, the first selection does not use the shadow effect, and the second does.

11 On page 3, format the heading as **24 pt**

Observe the Formatting differences box

Now only the Effects are different.

12 In the Reveal Formatting pane, click **Effects**

Click **Shadow**

In the Presets gallery, select the **No Shadow** icon

Click **Close**

The Reveal Formatting pane indicates that there are no more formatting differences.

13 Close the Reveal Formatting pane

14 Update and close the document

Topic B: Creating styles

This topic covers the following Microsoft Office Specialist objectives for exam 77-881: Word 2010.

#	Objective
2.1	**Apply font and paragraph attributes**
	2.1.2 Apply styles

This topic covers the following Microsoft Office Specialist objectives for exam 77-887: Word Expert 2010.

#	Objective
2.1	**Apply advanced font and paragraph attributes**
	2.1.2 Use character-specific styles

Using styles to apply formatting

Explanation

A *style* is a named set of formatting options (font, font size, font color, effects, and so on) that define the appearance of recurring text elements, such as headings or body text. By using a style, you can apply several formats in one step. For example, if you want all of the section titles in a document to be 16-point Cambria, you can apply the Heading 2 style to them. Using styles helps to maintain formatting consistency.

Applying styles

You can apply a style to selected text by selecting the desired style from the Styles gallery on the Home tab, shown in Exhibit 1-2. Word provides several built-in styles. For example, you can apply the Heading 1 style to format selected text as a heading. By default, in a new document, Word applies the Normal style to the entire document.

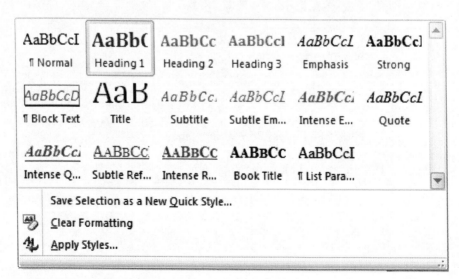

Exhibit 1-2: The Styles gallery

Quick Styles

A Quick Style is a set of styles that complement each other. By selecting a single Quick Style, you can format text easily to create an attractive, professional, and cohesive appearance. To apply a Quick Style set to a document:

1 On the Home tab, in the Styles group, click Change Styles.
2 Choose Style Set to display a list of Quick Styles.
3 Select the desired Quick Style set.

Do it!

B-1: Applying a style

The files for this activity are in Student Data folder **Unit 1\Topic B**.

Here's how	Here's why
1 Open Cookbook2	
Save the document as **My cookbook2**	In the current topic folder.
2 At the top of page 3, click in **The long history of spices**	You don't have to select the entire heading.
3 In the Styles group, click **Heading 1**	To apply the Heading 1 style to the page heading. This style formats the text as blue, bold, 16pt Cambria.
4 Click in the subheading **Introduction**	You'll apply a style to this text.
5 In the Styles group, click as shown	
	(The More button.) To display additional styles.
In the gallery, point to different styles	To preview the appearance of various styles. Each style applies a set of formats to the selected text.
6 In the gallery, select **Heading 2**	To apply the Heading 2 style to the subheading.
7 Update the document	

Creating styles by example

Explanation

You might have formatted some text by using a combination of options that you want to apply to other text. If you plan to use the same combination of formats repeatedly, you can create a style based on the formatting of selected text.

To create a style based on selected text:

1 Select the text on which you want to base the new style.

2 In the Styles group, click the Dialog Box Launcher to open the Styles pane, shown in Exhibit 1-3.

3 In the Styles pane, click the New Style button to open the Create New Style from Formatting dialog box, shown in Exhibit 1-4.

4 Enter a name for the new style.

5 Click OK or press Enter to use the selected formats and to create the style, which will now be available in the Styles gallery and the Styles list.

You can clear all formatting from selected text by clicking the Clear Formatting button in the Font group on the Home tab.

The Styles pane

You can use the Styles pane to create, modify, and apply styles. You can either create a style from scratch or modify an existing style and save it with a new name.

To apply a style by using the Styles pane, first select the text you want to format. Then, in the Styles list, select the desired style.

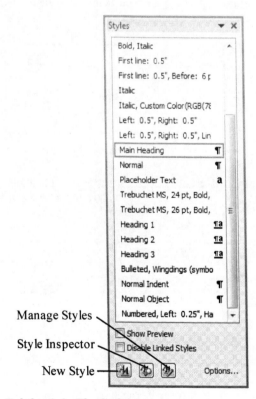

Exhibit 1-3: The Styles pane

Exhibit 1-4: The Create New Style from Formatting dialog box

Do it!

B-2: Creating a style by example

Here's how	Here's why
1 Select the heading **The long history of spices**	
In the Font group, click	(The Clear Formatting button.) To clear the formatting from the selected text.
Format the text as Arial Black, 18 pt, dark olive green	Use the options in the Font group. Select the Olive Green, Accent 3, Darker 50% color.
2 In the Styles group, click the Dialog Box Launcher	To open the Styles pane.
Click	(The New Style button.) To open the Create New Style from Formatting dialog box.
3 Edit the Name box to read **Main Heading**	
From the "Style based on" list, select **(no style)**	So that the new style does not inherit any style attributes from another style.
4 Click **OK**	To create the style. It appears in both the Styles pane and the Styles group. You'll now apply the new style to the other main headings in the document.
5 At the top of page 2, place the insertion point in **Contents**	
In the Styles group, click **Main Heading**	To apply the Main Heading style to the text.
6 Update the document	

Basing styles on other styles

Explanation

Another way to create a style is to base it on an existing style. The new style will inherit the formatting of the style it's based on, and any additional formats you select will either replace or be added to the inherited options. For example, suppose you create a section-heading style named "Appendix Heading." You want this style to have the same formatting as the Heading 1 style, but you want the text to be red. Rather than manually repeating the formatting of Heading 1, you can base the new style on it and then specify the red font color for the new style.

To base one style on another:

1 In the Styles pane, click the New Style button.

2 Enter a name for the new style.

3 From the "Style based on" list, select the style on which you want to base the new one.

4 Under Formatting, select any other formatting options that you want to include in the new style. Any formats you select will override the formatting of the "parent" style.

5 Click OK.

Do it!   **B-3:   Basing one style on another**

Here's how	Here's why
1 On page 3, place the insertion point in the text **Introduction**	
In the Styles pane, click **Clear All**	(At the top of the Styles list.) To clear the formatting from the text.
2 In the Styles pane, click [icon]	To open the Create New Style from Formatting dialog box.
3 Edit the Name box to read **Subheading 1**	
From the "Style based on" list, select **Main Heading**	This time, you do want the style to use another style's formats, plus those that you'll change.
4 From the Font Size list, select **14**	
From the Font Color list, select the red color	Red, Accent 2.
5 Click **OK**	To create the style and apply it to the text.
6 At the top of page 4, place the insertion point within **The medicinal use of spices**	
In the Styles pane, select **Subheading 1**	
7 On page 5, apply the **Subheading 1** style to **The spice trade**	
8 On page 4, place the insertion point within **Spices as ancient medicine**	
In the Styles pane, click the New Style button	
9 Name the style **Subheading 2**	
Base this style on Subheading 1	The new style will inherit formatting from Subheading 1, which, in turn, inherits formatting from Main Heading.
Set the font size to 12 pt	The new style will also use the italics and underlining already applied to the text.

10 Click **OK**

11 Apply the **Subheading 2** style   Click in the text and select Subheading 2 in the
to the following text: Styles pane.

On page 4: **Spices as modern
medicine**

On page 5: **A funny thing
happened on the way to
the Spice Lands...**

12 Update the document

More formatting options for styles

Explanation

In addition to font attributes, you can include other formatting options in a style. For example, you can use styles to apply paragraph, tab, and border formatting to text.

To select additional formatting options for a new style:

1 In the Create New Style from Formatting dialog box, click Format to show the additional options.
2 Select the kind of formatting you want to change.
3 Set the desired options, and then click OK to close the dialog box.
4 Click OK to save the settings.

Do it!

B-4: Controlling pagination by using styles

Here's how	Here's why
1 Move to page 6	For the spice names, you'll define a style that includes pagination control.
Place the insertion point in the heading **Bay leaf**	At the top of the page.
2 In the Styles pane, click the New Style button	
3 Name the style **Spice Name**	
Format the text as Trebuchet MS, 14 pt, bold	
4 Click **Format**	To display the Format menu.
Choose **Paragraph...**	To open the Paragraph dialog box.
Click the **Line and Page Breaks** tab	
Check **Page break before**	
5 Click **OK**	To close the Paragraph dialog box.
Click **OK**	To close the Create New Style from Formatting dialog box. Because there was already a page break before the spice name on this page, there is now an extra one.
6 Move to the top of page 6	(If necessary.) The page is blank.
Show the hidden formatting symbols	(In the Paragraph group, click the Show/Hide button.) The page-break symbol appears at the top of the page.
7 Select the page break	If necessary.
Press `DELETE`	To delete the manual page break. The page break that's included with the style does not appear as a formatting symbol in the document.
8 At the bottom of page 6, apply the **Spice Name** style to **Cinnamon**	Observe that the page breaks above the spice name after you apply the style.
9 Apply the **Spice Name** style to the remaining spice names	Cloves, Coriander, Cumin, Nutmeg, Pepper, Star anise, and Turmeric.
10 Update the document	

Character styles

Explanation

A character style is similar to a paragraph style, except that a character style applies to only the selected text, as shown in Exhibit 1-5, and it does not include paragraph formats. (A paragraph style can include both character and paragraph formats, and it applies to all text in a paragraph.) You can use a character style to format specific text without affecting the other text in the paragraph.

To create a character style:

1 Open the Create New Style from Formatting dialog box.
2 Name the style.
3 From the Style type list, select Character.
4 Select the desired formatting options.
5 Click OK.

Spicy Buzzard Wings
Category: Appetizer
Yield: 6 servings

Exhibit 1-5: A character style applied to the words "Category" and "Yield"

Do it!

B-5: Creating a character style

Here's how	Here's why
1 At the top of page 15, select **Category**	Below the text "Spicy Buzzard Wings."
2 In the Styles pane, click the New Style button	
3 Name the style **Label**	
From the Style type list, select **Character**	So that the style's formatting will be applied to selected characters, rather than to entire paragraphs.
Format the text as bold and dark red	
4 Click **Format** and choose **Border...**	To open the Borders and Shading dialog box.
Under Setting, click as shown	
	To apply a border to all four sides of the text.
5 Click the **Shading** tab	
From the Fill list, select the Olive Green, Accent 3 color	
6 Click **OK**	To close the Borders and Shading dialog box.
Click **OK**	
7 Select the word **Yield**	Under "Spicy Buzzard Wings."
In the Styles pane, select **Label**	To apply the character style.
8 Update and close the document	

Topic C: Modifying styles

This topic covers the following Microsoft Office Specialist objectives for exam 77-881: Word 2010.

#	Objective
2.1	**Apply font and paragraph attributes**
	2.1.1 Apply character attributes

This topic covers the following Microsoft Office Specialist objectives for exam 77-887: Word Expert 2010.

#	Objective
1.1	**Configure Word options**
	1.1.1 Change default program options
2.1	**Apply advanced font and paragraph attributes**
	2.1.1 Use character attributes

Updating styles

Explanation   One of the advantages of using styles is the ease with which you can make global changes. For example, if you change any of a style's properties, then all text formatted with that style automatically inherits the new properties. If your document contains multiple headings, subheadings, and other elements to which you've applied styles, this feature can be a big time-saver.

Managing styles

To modify a style, use the Modify Style dialog box. To open the Modify Style dialog box, do either of the following:

- In the Styles pane, point to the name of the style you want to modify. Click the down-arrow to the right of the style name and choose Modify.

- In the Styles pane, click the Manage Styles button to open the Manage Styles dialog box, shown in Exhibit 1-6. Select the name of the style you want to modify, and click Modify.

In the Modify Style dialog box, you can adjust the style's formatting just as you would in the Create New Style from Formatting dialog box.

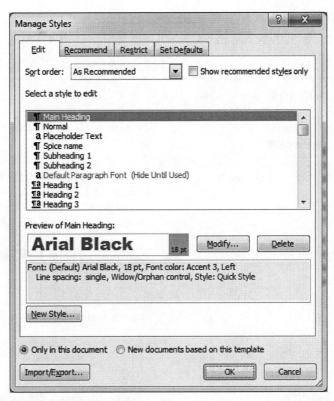

Exhibit 1-6: The Manage Styles dialog box

Automatically updating styles

You can have Word update a style automatically every time you apply manual formatting to text with that style applied. To do so, open the Modify Style dialog box for that style and check Automatically update.

Do it!

C-1:   Modifying a style

The files for this activity are in Student Data folder **Unit 1\Topic C**.

Here's how	Here's why
1 Open Cookbook3	
Save the document as **My cookbook3**	In the current topic folder.
2 Scroll through the document	To observe that text with the Main Heading, Subheading 1, and Subheading 2 styles all use the font Arial Black. You'll change the styles so that they all use Trebuchet MS.
3 Open the Styles pane	(If necessary.) In the Styles group, click the Dialog Box Launcher.
In the Styles pane, click [icon]	(The Manage Styles button.) To open the Manage Styles dialog box.
4 From the "Select a style to edit" list, select **Main Heading**	Scroll to the top of the list.
Click **Modify**	To open the Modify Style dialog box.
5 From the Font list, select **Trebuchet MS**	
6 Click **OK**	To return to the Manage Styles dialog box.
Click **OK**	To close the dialog box.
7 Observe the text on pages 3 and 4	The Main Heading, Subheading 1, and Subheading 2 styles now use the Trebuchet MS font, because Subheading 1 is based on Main Heading, and Subheading 2 is based on Subheading 1.
8 Update the document	

Overriding styles

There might be times when you want to change the formatting of text after applying a style to it. For example, after applying the Heading 1 style, you might decide to increase the heading font to 20 pt and change the case to small capital letters. When you manually format text that already has a style applied to it, you are *overriding* the style; the override is local and does not affect any other text with that style applied. When you override a style, the Styles pane lists a new style entry, consisting of the original style name followed by the additional formatting, such as "Main Heading + Small Caps," as shown in Exhibit 1-7.

Note: The automatic-update feature controls whether styles can be overridden. If you check Automatically update when defining a style, then any formatting you add will modify the style's global definition, rather than overriding the formatting locally.

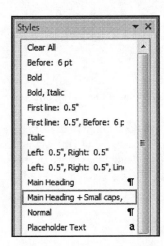

Exhibit 1-7: The Main Heading style, showing style overrides

Deleting styles

You can delete a style from a document by using the Styles pane. To do so, point to the name of the style you want to delete, click the down-arrow to the right of the style name, and choose Delete. When you delete a paragraph style, text that has been formatted with that style will revert to the Normal paragraph style.

Do it!   **C-2: Overriding a style**

Here's how	Here's why
1 On page 2, select **Contents**	You've applied the Main Heading style to this text, but you want to change its formatting without affecting any other text that uses the same style.
2 In the Font group, click the Dialog Box Launcher	To open the Font dialog box.
3 Check **Small caps**	
4 Click the **Advanced** tab	
From the Spacing list, select **Expanded**	
5 Click **OK**	To close the dialog box.
6 Observe the Styles pane	A description of the additional formatting appears next to the Main Heading style to indicate that you've overridden it.
7 Update the document	

The Normal style

Explanation

By default, when you create a document, Word applies the Normal style to the entire document. The Normal style uses the default settings for body text in a given document. All text uses the Normal style unless you have applied a different style to the text or formatted it manually. Also, Normal is the default "based on" style; therefore, changing the formatting for the Normal style can affect much of the formatting in your document.

Setting document defaults

You can change the default settings for a document by using the Manage Styles dialog box. To do so:

1 In the Styles pane, click the Manage Styles button.
2 Click the Set Defaults tab.
3 Select the desired settings and click OK.

By default, any changes you make in the default settings will be applied to only the current document.

Do it!

C-3: Modifying the Normal style

Here's how	Here's why
1 In the Styles pane, click [icon]	To open the Manage Styles dialog box. You'll change the formatting for the Normal style.
2 From the "Select a style to edit" list, select **Normal** Click **Modify**	
3 Click **Format** and choose **Paragraph...**	
4 Click the **Indents and Spacing** tab Under Indentation, set the Left value to **0.2"**	
5 Click **OK** three times	To close the dialog boxes.
6 On page 3, observe the text	The body text has the new indent settings. So does the text that uses the Spice Name style, because it was based on the Normal style. The other styles, not based on Normal, have their original indent settings.
7 Update the document	

Importing and exporting styles

Explanation
You can import styles from another document and export them from the current document. To import or export styles, follow these steps:

1 In the Manage Styles dialog box, click Import/Export to open the Organizer dialog box, shown in Exhibit 1-8. The styles available in the current document appear in the box on the left; by default, the styles in the Normal template appear on the right.

2 To import styles from or export styles to another document, click the Close File button on the right side of the dialog box; then click Open File.

3 Navigate to the folder containing the document with the styles you want to use.

4 From the file type list, select Word Documents.

5 Select the desired document and click Open.

6 Copy styles from one document or the other by selecting the appropriate style from the list and clicking Copy.

7 When you've finished copying styles, click Close.

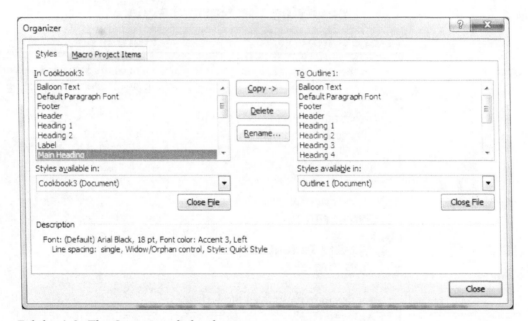

Exhibit 1-8: The Organizer dialog box

Do it!   ## C-4:   Exporting a style

The files for this activity are in Student Data folder **Unit 1\Topic C**.

Here's how	Here's why
1 In the Styles pane, click the Manage Styles button	You'll export a style from this document so that you can use it in another document.
2 Click **Import/Export**	To open the Organizer dialog box.
On the right side of the dialog box, click **Close File**	To close the Normal template. After you do this, the button changes to Open File.
Click **Open File**	To open the Open dialog box.
3 Navigate to the current topic folder	Because the default file type is Word templates, no documents appear.
From the file type list, select **All Word Documents**	
Select **Outline1**	From the Student Data folder for this topic.
Click **Open**	The right-hand list in the Organizer dialog box displays the styles available in Outline1.
4 From the list on the left, select **Main Heading**	
Click Copy ->	To copy the Main Heading style from the current document to Outline1.
5 Click **Close**	To close the dialog box. A warning box appears, asking if you want to save these changes.
Click **Don't Save**	You don't want to save changes at this time.
6 Close the Styles pane	
7 Update and close the document	

Topic D: Working with outlines

This topic covers the following Microsoft Office Specialist objectives for exam 77-881: Word 2010.

#	Objective
1.1	**Apply different views to a document.**
	1.1.4 Arrange document views
	1.1.4.1 Reorganize a document outline
2.2	**Navigate and search through a document**
	2.2.1 Use the Navigation Pane
	2.2.1.1 Headings
	2.2.1.2 Pages

Document outlines

Explanation

An *outline* provides a helpful way to view the main sections of a document. In Word, an outline consists of headings and subheadings that are formatted with an outline level. Outlines also help you with navigating in long documents because they enable you to collapse and expand text to view different levels.

Using styles to create an outline

When you format a document with Word's predefined heading or subheading styles, Word automatically creates an outline. You can switch to Outline view by clicking the Outline button in the Document Views group on the Views tab or by clicking the Outline button on the status bar.

When you switch to this view, the Outlining tab becomes available on the Ribbon. This tab has three groups: Outline Tools, Master Document, and Close.

To create an outline, you can apply the default styles Heading 1, Heading 2, and Heading 3 to text to create Level 1, Level 2, and Level 3 outline levels, as shown in Exhibit 1-9. You can also use the Outline Tools group, shown in Exhibit 1-10, to set and manipulate outline levels.

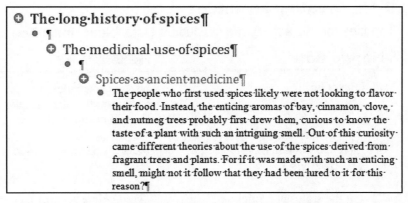

Exhibit 1-9: A document in Outline view, showing Level 1, Level 2, and Level 3 headings

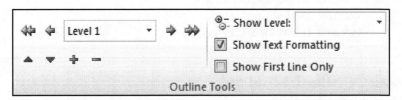

Exhibit 1-10: The Outline Tools group on the Outlining tab

The following table describes some of the commands in the Outline Tools group.

Button	Shortcut	Description
⇚		Promotes the selected text to the Heading 1 style (Level 1 outline level).
⇐	(ALT) + (SHIFT) + (←)	Promotes the selected text to the next highest outline level. If the text is already subordinate to an outline level, that text is promoted to the level to which it is subordinate.
⇒	(ALT) + (SHIFT) + (→)	Demotes the selected text to the next lowest outline level. If the text is already subordinate to an outline level, it is demoted to the next level below that to which it is subordinate.
⇛		Demotes the selected text to Body text.
▲	(ALT) + (SHIFT) + (↑)	Moves the selected paragraph up in the outline, without changing its outline level.
▼	(ALT) + (SHIFT) + (↓)	Moves the selected paragraph down in the outline, without changing its outline level.
✚	(ALT) + (+)	If collapsed, expands the selected outline level.
▬	(ALT) + _	If expanded, collapses the selected outline level.

Do it!

D-1: Creating an outline

The files for this activity are in Student Data folder **Unit 1\Topic D**.

Here's how	Here's why
1 Open Outline2	This document doesn't contain any formatting or styles (other than the Normal style). You'll use it to create an outline.
Save the document as **My outline2**	In the current topic folder.
2 On the status bar, click [icon]	(The Outline button.) To view the document as an outline. The Outlining tab appears on the Ribbon and is active.
3 At the top of page 1, place the insertion point within **A word from the chairman**	
In the Outline Tools group, from the Outline Level list, select **Level 1**	[Level 1 selector]
4 On page 2, place the insertion point within **Contents**	
Click [icon]	(The Promote to Heading 1 button.) To promote the text to Level 1 in the outline.
5 On page 3, promote **The long history of spices** to Level 1	Place the insertion point in the text and click the Promote to Heading 1 button.
6 Place the insertion point within **Introduction**	
Click [icon]	(The Demote button.) To demote the text to Level 2 in the outline.
7 On page 4, observe the text	All of the text after the Level 2 heading that you just created is subordinate to that heading. Thus, to set another Level 2 heading, you'll have to promote the desired text.
Place the insertion point within **The medicinal use of spices**	
Click [icon]	(The Promote button.) To promote the text one level higher, to Level 2.
8 On page 5, apply the Level 2 outline level to **The spice trade**	Place the insertion point in the text and click the Promote button.

9 On pages 4 and 5, apply Level 3 to the following phrases:
Spices as ancient medicine,
Spices as modern medicine, and
A funny thing happened on the way to the Spice Lands...

Place the insertion point in the text; then click the Demote button to set the first level ("Spices as ancient medicine"). Promote "Spices as modern medicine" to Level 3. For the third subheading, which is already subordinate to a Level 2 heading, click the Demote button.

10 Starting on page 6, apply Level 2 to each spice name

Bay leaf, Cinnamon, Cloves, Coriander, Cumin, Nutmeg, Pepper, Star anise, and Turmeric.

11 Starting on page 12, apply Level 2 to each recipe name

12 Update the document

Organizing outlines

Explanation

You can use Outline view to easily rearrange an outlined document. The plus sign next to an outline level indicates that there is additional text under the level heading, as shown in Exhibit 1-11. Double-click the plus sign to collapse the subordinate text under a level heading, and double-click it again to expand the text.

When you point to a plus sign in an outline, the pointer changes to a four-headed arrow, indicating that you can move the outline level. To do so, drag the plus sign to where you want the outline level—as well as any subordinate text—to appear in the outline. For long documents, organizing an outline might be easier with the outline levels collapsed. Alternatively, in the Outline Tools group, click Show First Line Only to show only the first line of each paragraph. Also, you can choose which levels to show by selecting an option from the Show Level list.

Exhibit 1-11: A document with outline levels collapsed

The Navigation pane

In addition to dragging outline levels in the document, you can use the Navigation pane to view and arrange a document outline. The Navigation pane displays document headings by outline level, as shown in Exhibit 1-12. To display this pane, click the View tab and check Navigation Pane in the Show group. To view an outline of document headings, click the "Browse the headings in your document" icon.

The Navigation pane can be helpful for navigating through a long document. As you move the insertion point in the document, corresponding headings on each page are highlighted in the Navigation pane. You can also click the headings in the Navigation pane to go directly to them in the document.

To rearrange headings in the Navigation pane, drag a heading to where you want it in the pane. A black line indicates where the heading and the text below it will appear.

Note: If you want to use the Navigation pane to browse headings, the document must contain heading styles or styles with outline levels defined.

Thumbnails

In Word, *thumbnails* are miniature images of the pages in a document. You can use thumbnails to easily navigate through a large document. To view document thumbnails, in the Navigation pane, click the "Browse the pages in your document" icon, shown in Exhibit 1-12. The page numbers also appear below the thumbnails.

As you move through the document, the Thumbnails pane updates to show the pages you're viewing. To navigate to a specific page, click its thumbnail image.

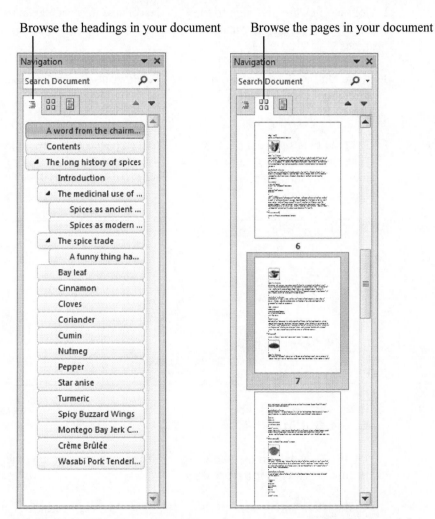

Exhibit 1-12: The Navigation pane, showing document headings and document pages

Do it!   **D-2:   Organizing an outline**

Here's how	Here's why
1 On page 4, double-click the plus sign to the left of "Spices as ancient medicine"	To collapse the text subordinate to that heading.
2 Double-click the plus sign to the left of "The medicinal use of spices"	To collapse the headings and text subordinate to that heading.
3 In the Outline Tools group, from the Show Level list, select **Level 3**	To view only Levels 1, 2, and 3 of the outline.
4 Drag the plus sign to the left of "The spice trade" so that it's above "The medicinal use of spices," as shown	In the screenshot below, notice the position of the mouse pointer (the vertical, double-headed arrow). This is the position you're dragging to.

⊕ The·long·history·of·spices¶
   ⊕ Introduction¶
────────────────────────────────── Page Break ──────
   ⊕ The·medicinal·use·of·spices¶
      ⊕ Spices·as·ancient·medicine¶
      ⊕ Spices·as·modern·medicine¶
────────────────────────────────── Page Break ──────
  ⊕ The·spice·trade¶
      ⊕ A·funny·thing·happened·on·the·way·to·the·Spice·Lands…¶
────────────────────────────────── Page Break ──────

5 In the Close group, click **Close Outline View**	To close Outline view. You can also organize an outline by using the Navigation pane.
6 On the View tab, in the Show group, check **Navigation Pane**	To open the Navigation pane.
In the Navigation pane, click [≡]	(The "Browse the headings in your document" icon.) If necessary, to see an outline of your document's headings in the Navigation pane.
7 In the Navigation pane, click as shown	

◢ The medicinal use of …
    Spices as ancient …
    Spices as modern …
  Bay leaf

To go to that heading in the document.

8 Drag the heading as shown

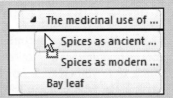

To move the heading and its subordinate text in the outline.

9 Close the Navigation pane

10 Update the document

Formatting text for an outline

Explanation

When you apply an outline level to text in Outline view, Word assigns that text a corresponding style. You can change the formatting for these styles just as you would for a style you created. For example, if you want all Level 1 headings to use the font Trebuchet MS, you can format the Heading 1 style to use that font. To change the formatting for an outline level, select the desired options in the corresponding style's Modify Style dialog box.

Alternatively, you can create a style, specify its outline level, and apply it to text to create an outline. For example, if you had a style named Main Heading, you could specify that it uses outline Level 1. Then when you apply that style to a heading, it will automatically be formatted as Level 1.

To set the outline level for a style:

1   In the Styles pane, click the Manage Styles button.

2   Select the style to which you want to assign an outline level, and click Modify.

3   Click Format and choose Paragraph.

4   Select an option from the Outline level list.

- For the Normal style, the default level is Body text. Any style based on Normal (the "based on" default) will also use the Body text level for outlining.

- For Heading 1, the default level is Level 1; for Heading 2, it's Level 2; and for Heading 3, it's Level 3.

- There are 10 outline levels: Body text, and Level 1 through Level 9.

5   Click OK.

Do it!   **D-3:   Formatting an outline**

Here's how	Here's why
1 Open the Styles pane	It displays the styles used in the outline (Normal for body text, and Heading 1, Heading 2, and Heading 3).
2 Click the Manage Styles button	To open the Manage Styles dialog box.
From the "Select a style to edit" list, select **Heading 1**	
Click **Modify**	
3 From the "Style based on" list, select **(no style)**	
Format the style as Trebuchet MS, 18 pt, bold, dark green	
Click **OK**	To return to the Manage Styles dialog box.
4 Modify the Heading 2 style so that it's based on Heading 1 and is Trebuchet MS, 16 pt, dark red	
5 Modify the Heading 3 style so that it's based on Heading 1 and is Trebuchet MS, 14 pt, black	
6 From the "Select a style to edit" list, select **Normal**	
Click **Modify**	
7 Click **Format** and choose **Paragraph...**	
Under Spacing, in the After box, click the up-arrow	To specify 6 points of space after the paragraph.
8 Click **OK** three times	To return to the document.
9 Close the Styles pane	
10 Update and close the document	

Unit summary: Styles and outlines

Topic A In this topic, you learned how to examine text formatting and compare the formatting of two selections by using the **Reveal Formatting** pane.

Topic B In this topic, you applied a **style** to some text. Then you learned how to create a style by example and how to base one style on another. Finally, you created a character style.

Topic C In this topic, you modified a style by using the **Manage Styles** dialog box, and you learned how to override a style. You also learned how to modify the Normal style. Finally, you **exported** a style to another document.

Topic D In this topic, you used styles to create an **outline**. Then you used Outline view and the Navigation pane to **organize** an outline. You also formatted an outline.

Independent practice activity

In this activity, you'll compare the styles of two selections and make them match. Then you'll create a style, apply it, use it to create a document outline, and view the outline.

The files for this activity are in Student Data folder **Unit 1\Unit summary**.

1 Open Practice styles and save it as **My practice styles**.

2 Use the Reveal Formatting pane to examine the formatting of the heading on page 1. (*Hint:* Press Shift+F1.)

3 Use the Reveal Formatting pane to format the heading on page 1 by using the same formatting options that are used for the heading on page 2.

4 Create a style named **Page heading**, based on the format of the heading on page 1.

5 Set the Page heading style to use outline Level 1.

6 Apply the Page heading style to the headings on pages 2, 3, 4, 5, 7, and 8.

7 View the document in Outline view, and then return to Print Layout view.

8 Display the Navigation pane, if necessary.

9 In the Navigation pane, view the document outline and thumbnails.

10 Close any open panes.

11 Update and close the document.

Review questions

1 What keys do you press to open the Reveal Formatting pane?

2 How do you use the Reveal Formatting pane to compare the formatting of two selections?

3 What are some advantages of using styles?

4 What style is applied to a new, blank document by default?

5 You've created a section-heading style named "Appendix Heading." You want this style to have the same formatting as the Heading 1 style, but you want the new style to make text red. How can you do this without manually specifying every style setting?

6 What happens if you check Automatically update in the Modify Style dialog box?

7 What happens if you delete a style that you've used in a document?

8 How can you use Word's predefined styles to create an outline?

9 If you want to create an outline from a document that uses custom styles, how can you do so?

10 How can you view and organize a document outline in Print Layout view?

Unit 2

Sections and columns

Unit time: 60 minutes

Complete this unit, and you'll know how to:

A Create and format sections of text by using section breaks, headers and footers, and page numbering.

B Format text into multiple columns.

Topic A: Creating and formatting sections

This topic covers the following Microsoft Office Specialist objectives for exam 77-881: Word 2010.

#	Objective
3.1	**Apply and manipulate page setup settings**
	3.1.1 Set margins
	3.1.7 Insert a section break
	3.1.7.1 Continuous
	3.1.7.2 Next page
	3.1.7.3 Next Odd
	3.1.7.4 Next Even
3.5	**Create and modify headers and footers**
	3.5.2 Format page numbers

This topic covers the following Microsoft Office Specialist objectives for exam 77-887: Word Expert 2010.

#	Objective
2.4	**Link sections**
	2.4.3 Link different sections

Section breaks

Explanation

Some page layout settings, such as margins and page numbering, typically apply to an entire document. Sometimes, though, you might want to use different layouts in different parts of a document. You can do this by dividing the document into sections.

A *section* is a portion of a document in which you can set certain page layout options, such as margins, headers and footers, page numbering, and page orientation. By default, a document has only one section. However, you can create additional sections in a document—and even on a single page—and apply different settings to each one.

To divide a document into sections, you need to insert section breaks. These are inserted as hidden formatting symbols, so they're visible only if the Show/Hide button is selected or if you're viewing the document in Draft or Outline view.

To insert a section break:

1 Place the insertion point where you want to create a new section.
2 On the Page Layout tab, in the Page Setup group, click Breaks to display the Breaks gallery, shown in Exhibit 2-1. Then choose a section break.

To delete a section break, place the insertion point just before it and press Delete.

There are four types of section breaks:

- **Next Page** — Starts a new section on the next page.
- **Continuous** — Starts a new section on the same page.
- **Even Page** — Starts a new section on the next even-numbered page.
- **Odd Page** — Starts a new section on the next odd-numbered page.

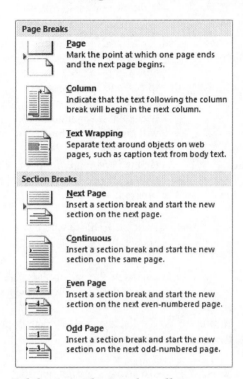

Exhibit 2-1: The Breaks gallery

Do it!

A-1: Inserting and deleting section breaks

The files for this activity are in Student Data folder **Unit 2\Topic A**.

Here's how	Here's why
1 Open Cookbook4	
Save the document as **My cookbook4**	In the current topic folder.
2 Scroll through the document	It begins with a letter from the chairman, followed by a table of contents, a history of spices, and spice descriptions, and ending with a collection of recipes. Each portion of the document is separated with page breaks. You will insert section breaks.
3 Show the hidden formatting symbols	(In the Paragraph group, click the Show/Hide button.) If necessary, to see the manual page breaks.
4 At the bottom of page 1, select the page break	(Click it.) This is where you'll insert the first section break.
Press [DELETE]	To delete the page break. The insertion point is now at the beginning of the heading "Contents."
5 On the Page Layout tab, in the Page Setup group, click **Breaks**	To display a gallery with options for page and section breaks.
Under Section Breaks, choose **Next Page**	To create a section that starts on the next page.
6 At the bottom of page 2, delete the page break	Click the page break to select it, and press Delete.
7 In the Page Setup group, click **Breaks** and choose **Next Page**	To create a new section.
	There are page breaks at the bottom of pages 3 and 4. You'll leave them there because pages 3, 4, and 5 are part of the same section.
8 On page 6, place the insertion point before "Bay leaf"	The Spice Name style is applied to this heading. The style includes formatting that inserts a page break before the heading automatically, so you can't delete the page break here.
Insert a Next Page section break	The section break replaces the page break.
9 Create a section that starts on page 15	(The page with the "Spicy Buzzard Wings" recipe.) Delete the page break on page 14, and insert a section break that starts the new section on the next page.
10 Update the document	

Section formatting

Explanation

You can apply different page layout settings to different sections. For example, you can change the orientation and apply different margins and borders to each section. To change the page layout for a section, first make sure the insertion point is in that section.

To change the page layout for an entire document when it contains sections:

1 Open the Page Setup dialog box.
2 From the Apply to list, select Whole document.
3 Specify the desired settings and click OK.

Do it!

A-2: Formatting sections

Here's how	Here's why
1 Press (CTRL) + (HOME)	To go to page 1, the first section in the document. You will set new margins for only this section.
2 In the Page Setup group, display the Margins gallery and select **Wide**	To change the left and right margins to 2 inches.
3 Scroll in the document	Notice that Word has applied the new margin settings to only the first section.
4 Place the insertion point in the first section	If necessary.
5 Click **Margins** and choose **Custom Margins...**	To open the Page Setup dialog box with the Margins tab active. You will specify custom margins.
6 Edit the Top box to read **2**	
Edit the Left box to read **1.25**	
Edit the Right box to read **1.25**	
In the Apply to list, verify that **This section** is selected	These changes will be applied to only the current section.
7 Click **OK**	To apply the margin settings.
8 Update the document	

Section headers and footers

Explanation

When you insert a header or footer in a section, that header or footer is applied by default to the entire document. For example, if you insert a header in the third section of a document with five sections, that header will appear in all five sections. To format the headers and footers differently for different sections, you have to remove the links between sections. To do so, activate the Header & Footer Tools | Design tab by editing either the header or the footer; then, in the Navigation group, click the Link to Previous button. Doing so removes the link between the current header or footer and the ones in previous sections. However, subsequent headers and footers (if any exist) will still be linked to the current one.

While headers and footers are linked, any text you type in one header or footer will appear in all headers or footers. After they are unlinked, you can edit and format them independently. However, any text you've already entered and any formatting you've already applied will remain in the other headers and footers until you change them.

To tell whether a section header or footer is linked, check the bottom-right corner of the header or footer area, as shown in Exhibit 2-2.

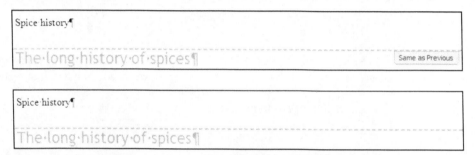

Exhibit 2-2: A linked header (top) and an unlinked header (bottom)

Do it!

A-3: Inserting section headers and footers

Here's how	Here's why
1 Go to page 3	This is the third section of the document, and it begins with the heading "The long history of spices."
2 On the Insert tab, in the Header & Footer group, click **Header** and choose **Edit Header**	To display the header area. The header is labeled "Header -Section 3-."
3 Type **Spice history**	
4 Observe the right side of the header	Same as Previous
	The text "Same as Previous" indicates that this section's header is linked to the header of the previous section. You'll remove the link so that you can edit each section's header separately.
5 In the Navigation group, click **Link to Previous**	To remove the link between the Section 3 header and the previous section header.

6 In the Navigation group, click **Previous**	To go to the previous section header, on page 2. Because you entered text in the header before you removed the link, that text appears in every header in the document.
Delete the contents of the header on page 2	
7 In the Navigation group, click **Previous**	To go to the header on page 1. Because the Section 1 and 2 headers are linked, when you deleted the text from the Section 2 header, the text in the Section 1 header was also deleted.
8 In the Navigation group, click **Next** three times	To go to the header on page 6, the fourth section of the document. This section's header is linked to the previous section's header, so the text you entered there appears here as well.
Remove the link to the previous section's header	In the Navigation group, click Link to Previous.
Edit the header text to read **Spice descriptions**	
9 In the Navigation group, click **Next**	To go to the header on page 15, the next section in the document.
Remove the link to the previous section's header	
Edit the header text to read **Recipes**	
10 Update the document	

Section page numbers

Explanation

Whenever you use the Insert Page Number command to insert page numbers, Word automatically inserts page numbers starting at 1 and continuing consecutively through a document. For some documents, however, you might need more complex numbering. For example, many books contain introductory material that is numbered with Roman numerals—"page 1" doesn't actually begin until several physical pages into the book.

You can tell Word how to format page numbers for different sections by using the Page Number Format dialog box, shown in Exhibit 2-3. Word can number linked sections consecutively but format them independently. For example, if you insert a page number in the first section—and that section is linked to the second section—then the page number will appear in the first and second sections. However, if you use the Page Number Format dialog box to change the number format for the first section, the formatting will apply to only the first section, and not the second. Likewise, if you insert page numbers in subsequent, unlinked sections, Word will continue numbering pages consecutively unless you specify otherwise in the Page Number Format dialog box.

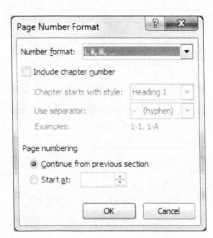

Exhibit 2-3: The Page Number Format dialog box

Do it!   **A-4:   Formatting section page numbers**

Here's how	Here's why
1 Move to the Section 1 header	You'll format this page and the contents page to use lowercase Roman numerals as page numbers.
2 On the Design tab, in the Header & Footer group, click **Page Number** and point to **Top of Page**	(Under Header & Footer Tools.) To display page number options.
Select **Plain Number 3**	To insert a page number on the right side of the header.
3 Click **Page Number** and choose **Format Page Numbers...**	(In the Header & Footer group.) To open the Page Number Format dialog box.
From the Number format list, select **i, ii, iii ...**	To use lowercase Roman numerals, commonly used to number introductory pages in books.
Click **OK**	To close the dialog box.
4 Move to the Section 2 header	
Observe the page number	Word inserted a page number here because this header is linked to the previous one. It's numbered consecutively, but the format didn't change because this is a separate section.
5 Click **Page Number** and choose **Format Page Numbers...**	In the Header & Footer group.
From the Number format list, select **i, ii, iii ...**	
Click **OK**	To format this section's page numbers as lowercase Roman numerals.
6 Move to the Section 3 header	(Section 3 begins on page 3.) You'll insert a page number and set it to use Arabic numerals.
Insert a page number with the style **Plain Number 3**	Click Page Number, choose Top of Page, and select the style.
	Notice that the current header text has been removed. You'll fix this.

7 Place the insertion point to the left of the page number and type **Spice history**	Click the left side of the header and type.
Press (TAB)	Spice·history → 3¶
Display the horizontal ruler	(If necessary.) On the View tab, in the Show group, check Ruler.
On the horizontal ruler, remove the Center Tab marker	To format the header so that the section title is aligned with the left margin, and the page number is aligned with the right margin.
8 Select the page number in the header	This page is numbered 3. You'll change the numbering to start with 1 on this page.
Open the Page Number Format dialog box	Click Page Number and choose Format Page Numbers.
Under Page numbering, select **Start at**	To have the page numbering start at page 1 in this section.
Click **OK**	
9 In Sections 4 and 5, insert a page number with the format **1, 2, 3, …**	Section 4 begins on page 6, and Section 5 begins on page 15. When you insert the page numbers, the first page in Section 4 will be numbered as page 4, and the first page in Section 5 will be numbered as page 13.
	When you insert a page number, Word deletes the existing header text. You'll need to reformat the header as described in the steps above.
10 Double-click in the document area	To close the header and footer areas.
11 Update and close the document	

Topic B: Working with columns

This topic covers the following Microsoft Office Specialist objectives for exam 77-881: Word 2010.

#	Objective
3.1	**Apply and manipulate page setup settings**
	3.1.3 Add hyphenation
	3.1.4 Add columns
	3.1.5 Remove a break
	3.1.7 Insert a section break
	3.1.7.1 Continuous

Formatting text into columns

Explanation

Newsletters, brochures, and reports often present content in columns. Using columns can save space by enabling you to present more information on a page, as shown in Exhibit 2-4. This can help reduce the page count of a long document.

To format text into columns:

1   Select the text you want to format as columns. (Drag to select the text; or if you want to format an entire section, place the insertion point anywhere in that section.)

2   On the Page Layout tab, in the Page Setup group, click Columns and choose More Columns to open the Columns dialog box, shown in Exhibit 2-5.

3   Under Presets, select a format. If you need more than three columns, enter the value in the Number of columns box.

4   Adjust the width and spacing of the columns as needed. (As you change the various settings in this dialog box, observe the Preview area to get an idea of how the selected text will look.)

5   Click OK.

You can also create columns by using the options in the Columns gallery in the Page Setup group.

Hyphenation

Often, when you format text into columns, you'll find that the text doesn't seem to fit as well. If you haven't enabled hyphenation, Word will attempt to fit the text into the given space, but there might be large gaps between words (if the text is justified) or unusually ragged edges (if the text is left- or right-aligned). You can improve the appearance and readability of the text by turning hyphenation on.

To enable hyphenation, click the Page Layout tab; in the Page Setup group, click Hyphenation and select Automatic. To specify more settings for how Word hyphenates, click Hyphenation and choose Hyphenation Options.

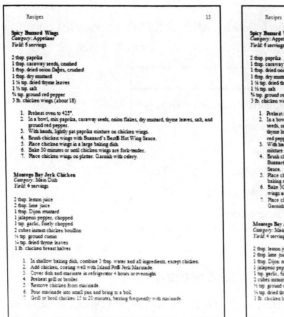

Exhibit 2-4: Text in a single column (left) and two columns (right)

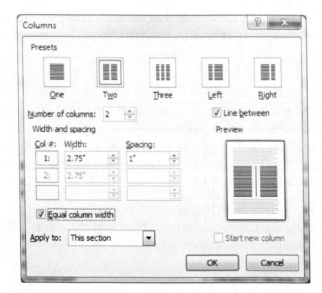

Exhibit 2-5: The Columns dialog box

Adjusting the spacing between columns

You can adjust the spacing between columns to provide balance. For example, if the columns are too close together, the text might be difficult to read. To adjust the spacing:

1 Select the columns between which you want to adjust the spacing.

2 Open the Columns dialog box.

3 Under Width and spacing, in the Spacing box, enter the desired measurement (in inches). The Width box adjusts to accommodate the new spacing.

4 Click OK.

Do it!   **B-1:   Formatting text into columns**

The files for this activity are in Student Data folder **Unit 2\Topic B**.

Here's how	Here's why
1 Open Cookbook5	
Save the document as **My cookbook5**	In the current topic folder.
2 Place the insertion point in any of the recipes	In the last section of the document, beginning on page 15 (numbered as page 13).
3 On the Page Layout tab, in the Page Setup group, click **Columns**	To display the Columns gallery.
Select **Two**	To have the text flow into two columns.
4 Scroll through the document	The column settings were applied to the last section only.
5 Place the insertion point in the last section of the document	If necessary.
Display the Margins gallery and select **Normal**	To narrow the left and right margins in this section.
6 Click **Columns** and choose **More Columns...**	
Check **Line between**	To add a vertical line between the columns.
Edit the Spacing box for column 1 to read **1**	Width and spacing Col #: Width: Spacing: 1: 3" 1
	To set the space between the columns to 1 inch.
Press TAB	Notice that the column width changes when you set a new Spacing value.
7 Click **OK**	To apply the column settings.
8 In the Page Setup group, click **Hyphenation** and choose **Automatic**	Word applies hyphenation to the entire document. Some of the text re-flows.
9 Update the document	

Inserting and deleting column breaks

Explanation

A *column break* is a mark that indicates the end of a column. When one of the columns is longer than another, you can insert a column break to balance them. The text after the break will move to the next column. You might also want to start a paragraph at the beginning of a column or move a heading to the next column to improve readability.

To insert a column break:

1 Place the insertion point where you want to insert the column break.

2 Click the Page Layout tab.

3 In the Page Setup group, click Breaks and choose Column.

To delete a column break, place the insertion point just before the break and press Delete. When the column break is deleted, the text shifts to the previous column.

Do it!

B-2: Inserting column breaks

Here's how	Here's why
1 On page 15, place the insertion point to the left of "Montego Bay Jerk Chicken"	The second recipe, in the left column. You want the recipe names to appear at the top of each column.
2 On the Page Layout tab, in the Page Setup group, click **Breaks** and select **Column**	To insert a column break. The text after the insertion point moves to the right column.
3 On page 15, insert a column break before "Big D Veggie Chili"	Place the insertion point. Click Breaks and select Column.
4 Insert column breaks before the Crème Brûlée and Wasabi Pork Tenderloin recipes	
5 Update the document	

Creating a heading that spans columns

Explanation

Even though you have text laid out in columns, you might want a heading that stretches across all of them, instead of across just one column. To add a heading that spans columns and uses the width of the page:

1 Place the insertion point where you want the heading to appear, and type the heading text.

2 Insert a Continuous section break after the text.

3 Place the insertion point in the section with the heading.

4 Set the number of columns to one.

Do it!

B-3: Adding a heading across columns

Here's how	Here's why
1 On page 15, place the insertion point to the left of "Spicy Buzzard Wings" Type **Cooking with Outlander Spices**	
2 From the Breaks gallery, select **Continuous**	To create a section break that doesn't break across pages or columns.
3 Press (←)	To move the insertion point to the end of the heading you just typed.
4 Set the number of columns to 1	(In the Columns gallery, select One.) To make the heading span both columns.
Press (← ENTER) twice	To insert a blank line after the heading.
5 Place the insertion point in the line **Cooking with Outlander Spices** Center the text horizontally	(On the Home tab, in the Paragraph group, click the Center button.) The heading uses one column instead of two.
6 Update and close the document	

Unit summary: Sections and columns

Topic A   In this topic, you learned how to insert and delete **section breaks**. Then you formatted pages in a section. Next, you inserted section **headers and footers**. You also formatted section page numbers.

Topic B   In this topic, you formatted text into **columns**. You learned how to insert column breaks, and you added a heading that spans multiple columns.

Independent practice activity

In this activity, you'll create sections in a document. Then you'll insert page numbers and format them in different sections. You'll also format some text into columns.

The files for this activity are in Student Data folder **Unit 2\Unit summary**.

1 Open Practice sections and save it as **My practice sections**.

2 Create sections that begin on pages 2, 3, 4, 5, 7, and 8.

3 In the header section of each page, insert the page number on the right side.

4 Format the page number for page 1 as a lowercase Roman numeral. (*Hint:* First, remove the link between this section and the next.)

5 Format the page numbering to begin at 1, starting on the second page of the document.

6 In the section that begins on page 8 (Section 7), format the text into two columns.

7 Insert a column break so that page 8 appears as shown in Exhibit 2-6.

8 Format the heading on page 8 so that it spans both columns. (*Hint:* After you insert the section break, an extra paragraph mark will appear in the first column; delete it.)

9 Update and close the document.

7¶

¶
SPICE·TIPS¶

Store·spices·in·a·cool,·dark·place.· Humidity,·light,·and·heat·will·cause· herbs·and·spices·to·lose·their·flavor· more·quickly.··Although·the·most· convenient·place·for·your·spice·rack· may·be·above·your·stove,·moving·your· spices·to·a·different·location·may·keep· them·fresh·longer.¶

As·a·general·rule,·herbs·and·ground· spices·will·retain·their·best·flavors·for·a· year.·Whole·spices·may·last·for·3·to·5· years.·Proper·storage·will·result·in· longer·freshness·times.¶

························Column Break························

When·possible,·grind·whole·spices·in·a· grinder·or·mortar·&·pestle·just·prior·to· using.·Toasting·whole·spices·in·a·dry· skillet·over·medium·heat·before· grinding·will·bring·out·even·more·flavor.· Be·careful·not·to·burn·them!¶

Because·the·refrigerator·is·a·humid· environment,·you·shouldn't·refrigerate· herbs·and·spices.·To·keep·large· quantities·of·spices·fresh,·store·them·in· the·freezer·in·tightly·sealed·containers.¶

Exhibit 2-6: Page 8 as it appears after Step 7

Review questions

1 Why might you want to create sections?

2 What are the four types of section breaks?

3 Your document is divided into five sections, and you want to create a header in the third section. By default, any text that you enter is applied to the headers in which of the following?

   A Any sections that come after the current section

   B Any sections that come before the current section

   C Only the current section

   D Every section in the document

4 How do you change the spacing between columns?

5 How do you position a heading so that it spans columns?

Unit 3
Formatting tables

Unit time: 60 minutes

Complete this unit, and you'll know how to:

A Align text in a table, merge and split table cells, change text orientation in a table, and resize rows.

B Change table borders and apply shading to cells.

C Sort data in a table, split a table, repeat a header row on multiple pages, and enter a formula in a table.

D Apply and modify table styles.

Topic A: Table formatting basics

This topic covers the following Microsoft Office Specialist objectives for exam 77-881: Word 2010.

#	Objective
2.6	**Manipulate tables in a document**
	2.6.4 Manipulate rows
	2.6.4.1 Split
	2.6.4.2 Merge
	2.6.5 Manipulate columns
	2.6.5.1 Split
	2.6.5.2 Merge
	2.6.5.4 Resize

Table formatting options

Explanation

Because tabular information is sometimes difficult to read, some formatting might help to direct your audience's attention to particular areas of a table, making it easier for them to follow and process the information. For example, you can align text in cells, merge cells, apply borders and shading to cells, and change text orientation.

Aligning table text

When you enter text in a table cell, Word aligns the text with the upper-left corner by default. You can change text alignment by using buttons in the Alignment group, shown in Exhibit 3-1, on the Table Tools | Layout tab. You can change the text alignment for every cell in a table or for only selected cells. To change the alignment for a selected cell, place the insertion point in the cell and click one of the alignment buttons in the Alignment group. To change the text alignment for every cell in a table, select the table and select an alignment option.

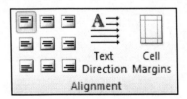

Exhibit 3-1: The Alignment group on the Table Tools | Layout tab

Do it!   **A-1:   Aligning text in table cells**

The files for this activity are in Student Data folder **Unit 3\Topic A**.

Here's how	Here's why
1 Open Kiosk locations1	
Save the document as **My kiosk locations1**	In the current topic folder.
2 Select the top row of the table	(Point to the left of the row and click to select the header row.) The Table Tools tabs appear on the Ribbon.
3 Click the **Layout** tab	Under Table Tools.
In the Alignment group, click ☰	(The Align Center Left icon.) To center the text in the header row vertically and have it left-aligned horizontally.
4 Select the cells containing the numbers in the table's right column, as shown	Projected· Revenues¶ ($·in·thousands)¤ 47¤ 62¤ 56¤ 71¤ 102¤ 83¤ 40¤ 38¤ 165¤ 95¤ 88¤ 132¤ 52¤ 53¤ 27¤
On the Layout tab, click ☰	(The Align Center icon.) To center the text.
5 Update the document	

Merging cells

Explanation

When you present your data in a table, you might want some cells to span more than one column or row. You do this by *merging* cells: combining two or more adjacent cells to form a single cell. For example, you might have empty cells that you want to merge into one cell; doing so makes a table less "busy" and helps direct your audience's attention to important information.

To merge cells in a table, select the cells you want to merge. Then, on the Table Tools | Layout tab, click Merge Cells in the Merge group. You can also right-click the selected cells and choose Merge Cells from the shortcut menu.

Do it!   **A-2:   Merging table cells**

Here's how	Here's why
1 In the first cell of the third row, delete **MD**	(Below the first MD row.) Three cells contain the same information. You'll delete the redundant text and merge the cells into one.
2 In the first cell of the fourth row, delete **MD**	
3 Select the three cells as shown	
In the Merge group, click **Merge Cells**	(On the Table Tools | Layout tab.) To merge the three cells into one. It's now easier to see which cities are in Maryland.
4 Delete **NJ** from the second and third NJ cells	
5 Merge the three cells, as shown	Select the three cells, and in the Merge group, click Merge Cells.
6 Remove the remaining duplicate state abbreviations, and merge the cells for each state, as shown	

7 Update the document

Splitting cells

Explanation

You might also need to *split* a cell, dividing it into two or more cells, creating new rows and/or columns. For example, if you need to add a cell to a section of a table, but you don't want to add an entire row or column, you can split a cell.

To split a cell:

1   Place the insertion point in the cell you want to split.

2   On the Table Tools | Layout tab, in the Merge group, click Split Cells.

3   Enter the number of columns and rows you want to create from the selected cell.

4   Click OK.

Do it!

A-3:   Splitting table cells

Here's how	Here's why
1 Place the insertion point in the first column	You want to insert a column that will list the sales manager for each state.
2 On the Table Tools	Layout tab, in the Rows & Columns group, click **Insert Right**	Word inserts a column with the number of rows corresponding with the layout of the table before the cells in the left column were merged.
	Rather than merging each group of cells to correspond with the states, you want to create a column that has the same layout as the State column.
Press CTRL + Z	To undo the last action.
3 Select the State column	(Be sure to select the entire column.) You'll split each cell in the column into two, in effect creating a new column that corresponds with the layout of the State column.
4 In the Merge group, click **Split Cells**	To open the Split Cells dialog box.
Verify that the Number of columns box reads **2**	After the split, you'll have two columns.
Clear **Merge cells before split**	If you don't clear this option, Word will merge the cells in the State column and divide the contents into two cells.
	The Number of rows box becomes dimmed.
Click **OK**	To split the cells.
5 In the top cell of the new column, type **Sales Manager**	
6 Update the document	

Changing the orientation of text

Explanation   To improve the readability of data in a table, you might need to change its orientation. By default, Word aligns text horizontally. To change the orientation of text in a table:

1 Select the cell(s) whose orientation you want to change.

2 On the Table Tools | Layout tab, in the Alignment group, click Text Direction.

- If the text is originally displayed horizontally (read from left to right), then clicking once will change the orientation to vertical (read from top to bottom).

- Clicking twice will switch the direction of the vertical orientation so that the text is read from bottom to top.

- Clicking a third time will restore the text to its original position.

Do it!   ## A-4:   Changing text orientation

Here's how	Here's why
1 Place the insertion point in any cell in the first column	
On the Table Tools | Layout tab, in the Rows & Columns group, click **Insert Left**	To add a new column to the left of the table. Word automatically selects the new column.
2 Merge all of the cells in the column	In the Merge group, click Merge Cells.
3 In the left column, type **Mid-Atlantic Region Kiosks**	
4 In the Alignment group, click **Text Direction** twice	The text now flows vertically from the bottom to the top of the column.
5 In the Alignment group, click ⫿	(The Align Center icon.) Note that the icons in the Alignment group have changed to reflect the new text direction.
In the Cell Size group, from the AutoFit list, select **AutoFit Contents**	To adjust the table so its contents fit in the adjusted layout.
6 Update the document	

Resizing rows

Explanation

By default, Word automatically adjusts the size of a cell to fit its contents, but you might want to increase or decrease a cell's default size. You can change the size of table rows by dragging the cell boundaries or by changing the settings in the Cell Size group.

To change the row height, point to the row boundary; when the pointer becomes a double-headed arrow, drag up or down. To specify a row's height precisely, first place the insertion point in the row whose height you want to change. Then, in the Cell Size group, enter a value in the Height box.

Do it!

A-5: Changing row height

Here's how	Here's why
1 Select the cells in the header row	Do not include the left column of merged cells.
2 In the Cell Size group, edit the Table Row Height box to read **0.5** and press ⏎ ENTER	Height: 0.5 Width:
	To decrease the row height.
	A message box appears, stating that the cell height can't be greater than the page height.
Click **OK**	To close the message box.
3 Select the cells with the city, store location, and revenue information, as shown	

City¤	Store·Location¤	Projected·Revenues¶ ($·in·thousands)¤
Baltimore¤	Prestige·Market¤	47¤
Bethesda¤	Prestige·Market¤	62¤
Rockville¤	Mediterranean·Gourmet¤	56¤
Atlantic·City¤	Roma¤	71¤
Cherry·Hill¤	Patterson's·Grocers¤	102¤
Trenton¤	Roma¤	83¤
Albany¤	Prestige·Market¤	40¤
Buffalo¤	Mediterranean·Gourmet¤	38¤
New·York¤	Patterson's·Grocers¤	165¤
New·York¤	Village·Gourmet·Bakery·and·Grocer¤	95¤
Harrisburg¤	Patterson's·Grocers¤	88¤
Philadelphia¤	Patterson's·Grocers¤	132¤
Charlottesville¤	Roma¤	52¤
Fairfax¤	Mediterranean·Gourmet¤	53¤
Richmond¤	Prestige·Market¤	27¤

Here's how	Here's why
In the Cell Size group, next to the Table Row Height box, click the up-arrow to make the value **0.3**	All of the selected rows change, as well as the merged cells containing the state abbreviations.
4 Update and close the document	

Topic B: Borders and shading

Explanation

After you've created a table, you can apply borders and shading to highlight cells, rows, columns, or the entire table. By using the formatting options in the Table Styles and Draw Borders groups, you can apply borders of different widths and styles, and you can apply borders to different areas of a table. You can also apply shading of different colors to selected cells.

Table borders

To apply borders:

1. Select the cells you want to apply the border to, or select the entire table.
2. On the Table Tools | Design tab, select options in the Draw Borders group:
   - From the Line Style list, select a border style.
   - From the Line Weight list, select a thickness.
   - From the Pen Color list, select a color.
3. In the Table Styles group, choose an option from the Borders menu, shown in Exhibit 3-2, to apply the border with the selected formatting to specific areas of the table.

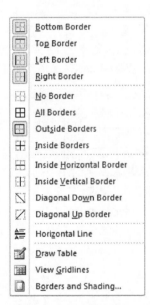

Exhibit 3-2: The Borders menu

Do it!

B-1: Changing table borders

The files for this activity are in Student Data folder **Unit 3\Topic B**.

Here's how	Here's why
1 Open Kiosk locations2	
Save the document as **My kiosk locations2**	In the current topic folder.
2 Select the indicated cells	

	State¤	Sales-Manager¤	City¤	Store·Location¤	Projected-Revenues¶ ($·in·thousands)¤
Mid-Atlantic·Region·Kiosks¤	MD¤	¤	Baltimore¤	Prestige·Market¤	47¤
			Bethesda¤	Prestige·Market¤	62¤
			Rockville¤	Mediterranean·Gourmet¤	56¤
	NJ¤	¤	Atlantic·City¤	Roma¤	71¤
			Cherry·Hill¤	Patterson's·Grocers¤	102¤
			Trenton¤	Roma¤	83¤
	NY¤	¤	Albany¤	Prestige·Market¤	40¤
			Buffalo¤	Mediterranean·Gourmet¤	38¤
			New·York¤	Patterson's·Grocers¤	165¤
			New·York¤	Village·Gourmet·Bakery·and·Grocer¤	95¤
	PA¤	¤	Harrisburg¤	Patterson's·Grocers¤	88¤
			Philadelphia¤	Patterson's·Grocers¤	132¤
	VA¤	¤	Charlottesville¤	Roma¤	52¤
			Fairfax¤	Mediterranean·Gourmet¤	53¤
			Richmond¤	Prestige·Market¤	27¤

Here's how	Here's why
3 Click the **Design** tab	Under Table Tools.
In the Draw Borders group, display the **Line Weight** list and select **2 1/4 pt**	
4 In the Table Styles group, display the **Borders** menu and choose **Outside Borders**	
5 Click in the left column of the table	(The column with the vertical text.) You will remove the border from the top, bottom, and left sides of the column.
6 In the Draw Borders group, from the Line Style list, select **No Border**	

7 In the Table Styles group, from the Borders menu, choose **Top Border**	To remove the top border.
From the Borders menu, choose **Left Border**	To remove the left border.
From the Borders menu, choose **Bottom Border**	To remove the bottom border.
8 Update the document	

Cell shading

Explanation

You might want to highlight some sections of a table to visually differentiate them from other sections, as shown in Exhibit 3-3. You can apply shading to do so. You can apply shading to the entire table or to specific cells. First select the cells you want to shade. Then, on the Table Tools | Design tab, in the Table Styles group, select a color in the Shading gallery.

State	Sales Manager	City	Store Location	Projected Revenues ($ in thousands)
MD		Baltimore	Prestige Market	47
		Bethesda	Prestige Market	62
		Rockville	Mediterranean Gourmet	56

Exhibit 3-3: Shaded cells in a table

Do it!

B-2: Shading table cells

Here's how	Here's why
1 Select the cells in the header row	
2 On the Table Tools | Design tab, in the Table Styles group, display the Shading gallery and select the indicated green color	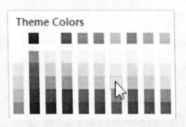 Olive Green, Accent 3, Lighter 40%.
3 Select the cells below "Projected Revenues"	
4 In the Shading gallery, select a color to shade the cells	In the Table Styles group.
5 Update and close the document	

Topic C: Table data

This topic covers the following Microsoft Office Specialist objectives for exam 77-881: Word 2010.

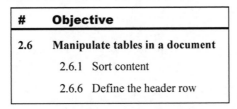

#	Objective
2.6	**Manipulate tables in a document**
	2.6.1 Sort content
	2.6.6 Define the header row

This topic covers the following Microsoft Office Specialist objectives for exam 77-887: Word Expert 2010.

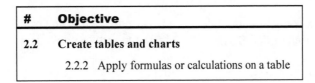

#	Objective
2.2	**Create tables and charts**
	2.2.2 Apply formulas or calculations on a table

Working with table data

Explanation

Tables in Word have some of the same functionality as tables in Excel. For example, you can sort data, and you can insert equations in table cells. For more complex operations, however, you should use a spreadsheet program like Excel.

Sorting data in a table

You can use the Sort command to organize table information in a particular order. To do so, first select the rows to be organized. Then, on the Table Tools | Layout tab, in the Data group, click Sort to open the Sort dialog box, shown in Exhibit 3-4. By default, the selected data is sorted alphabetically in ascending order. You can also sort numerically or chronologically.

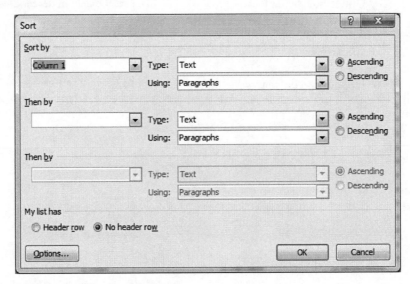

Exhibit 3-4: The Sort dialog box

Do it!

C-1:   Sorting table data

The files for this activity are in Student Data folder **Unit 3\Topic C**.

Here's how	Here's why
1 Open Sorting	
Save the document as **My sorting**	In the current topic folder.
2 Observe the table data	The states and cities aren't listed in alphabetical order.
3 Select all of the table rows except the header row	
On the Table Tools | Layout tab, in the Data group, click **Sort**	To open the Sort dialog box. You'll sort first by state and then by city.
4 From the Sort by list, select **Column 1**	(If necessary.) To have the table rows sorted initially by state.
From the Then by list, select **Column 2**	To have the table rows within each state sorted by city.
Click **OK**	To sort the table data.
5 In the Data group, click **Sort**	
In the Sort by list, select **Column 3**	Number appears in the Type box because the information in column 3 is numeric.
From the Then by list, select **(none)**	You no longer want to perform a secondary sort on Column 2 data.
Under Sort by, select **Descending**	To sort the data in descending order by the values in column 3.
Click **OK**	
6 Update and close the document	

Splitting tables

Explanation

You might be working with one table that you want to split into two. For example, you might want to sort different sections of a table or show sections separately, with text in between. To split a table:

1. Place the insertion point where you want to split the table. The selected row will be the first row of the new table.
2. On the Table Tools | Layout tab, in the Merge group, click Split Table.

Do it!

C-2:   Splitting a table

The files for this activity are in Student Data folder **Unit 3\Topic C**.

Here's how	Here's why
1 Open Split table	
Save the document as **My split table**	(In the current topic folder.) The table contains data from Eastern and Western states. You'll split the table so that you can sort data for each region separately.
2 Click the cell containing WA	You'll split the table into eastern and western regional tables.
On the Table Tools | Layout tab, in the Merge group, click **Split Table**	To split the table, with the selected row becoming the top row of the new table.
3 Copy the header from the first table	Select the three cells containing the column headings and press Ctrl+C.
In the second table, place the insertion point in the WA cell	You'll paste the header you just copied. Word will paste the copied cells above the current row.
Press CTRL + V	
4 Update and close the document	

Repeating a header row on multiple pages

Explanation

When you have a table that spans multiple pages, you probably want the header row to appear at the top of each page. In Word, the *header row* is the first row in a table, and typically it contains descriptive headings for the data in each column. If the header row appears at the top of each page, people reading the table don't have to flip back to the first page to determine which column they're viewing. However, if you add or remove rows or format the table differently, you'll still want the header to appear at the top of each page, rather than to re-flow with the rest of the table.

To do this, make sure that the header you want to use is the top row of the table. Then, with that row selected, click the Table Tools | Layout tab and click Repeat Header Rows in the Data group. You can also open the Table Properties dialog box, click the Row tab, and check "Repeat as header row at the top of each page."

Do it! **C-3: Repeating the header row**

The files for this activity are in Student Data folder **Unit 3\Topic C**.

Here's how	Here's why
1 Open Repeat header	
Save the document as **My repeat header**	In the current topic folder.
2 Scroll to examine the table	The data continues onto a second page. You want the header to appear at the top of each new page that contains this table.
Return to the top of the document	
3 Place the insertion point in the empty row below "Sales report"	You'll split the table so that the next row is the header row. Word automatically identifies the top row of a table as the header.
Split the table	On the Table Tools | Layout tab, in the Merge group, click Split Table.
4 Select the empty row at the top of the second table	Point to it in the selection bar and click.
Press (← BACKSPACE)	To delete the empty row.

Outlander·Spices¶ Sales·report¤				¤
¶				
Product¤	**Region¤**	**Prior·year¤**	**Current·year¤**	¤
Annatto·Seed¤	East¤	$11,771¤	$24,181¤	¤

5 Place the insertion point in the header row of the second table	(If necessary.) The header row contains the Product, Region, Prior year, and Current year cells.
6 On the Table Tools | Layout tab, in the Data group, click **Repeat Header Rows**	
7 Move to page 2	The header appears at the top of the page. If you added rows to or removed rows from the first page of the table, the header would still appear at the top of this page, as long as the table continued onto it.
8 Update and close the document	

Using the Formula dialog box

Explanation

You can perform various calculations in rows and columns by using formulas. A *formula* is used to perform arithmetic operations, such as calculating an average or a sum. You can also copy formulas from one cell to another in a table.

You can create formulas by using the Formula dialog box, shown in Exhibit 3-5. To open the Formula dialog box, click the Table Tools | Design tab and click Formula in the Data group. In the Formula dialog box:

- A formula is always preceded by an equal sign (=).
- From the Number format list, you can select the format in which you want the result displayed, such as currency or a percentage.
- From the Paste function list, select the function you want to use in the formula. A *function* is a built-in formula used to perform mathematical calculations. For example, the SUM function adds the numbers in the selected cells.

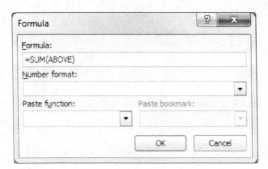

Exhibit 3-5: The Formula dialog box

In Word documents, formulas are treated as fields. When information is subject to change, a *field* is used as a placeholder for that information. For example, a formula that totals a column of numbers is based on the values in the column. If any number in the column changes, the formula needs to reflect the change. In such situations, fields provide the best way to store and display dynamic information.

Calculating totals in rows and columns

Use the SUM function to calculate totals in rows and columns. If the insertion point is in a table containing a series of numbers, the SUM function appears in the Formula dialog box by default. If the insertion point is placed below a cell containing a number, the Formula box will contain =SUM(ABOVE), which adds the numbers in the column. By default, the formula result will have the same formatting as the numbers used in the calculation.

Do it!   **C-4:   Entering a formula in a table**

The files for this activity are in Student Data folder **Unit 3\Topic C**.

Here's how	Here's why
1 Open Quarterly sales1	
Save the document as **My quarterly sales1**	In the current topic folder.
2 In the first table, place the insertion point in the bottom cell of the North America column	The cell is empty.
On the Table Tools | Layout tab, in the Data group, click **Formula**	To open the Formula dialog box. You'll use the default formula.
Click **OK**	To insert a field that calculates the sum of the cells above the selected cell.
3 In the first table, place the insertion point in the bottom cell of the Europe column	
In the Data group, click **Formula**	
Click **OK**	
4 Insert a sum formula for Pacific Rim sales	
5 Update and close the document	

Topic D: Table styles

Explanation

You already know that you can apply styles to paragraphs by using the Styles gallery. Similarly, you can apply styles to tables by using the Table Styles gallery on the Table Tools | Design tab. Word provides several style formats you can use to display information in different kinds of tables.

Applying styles to tables

You might want to highlight specific columns or rows, or you might want to shade alternate columns or rows to make reading the data easier. You can do this manually, but you might also be able to use one of Word's table styles, shown in Exhibit 3-6.

To apply a style to a table, first place the insertion point in the table. Then, in the Table Styles group, select a style from the Table Styles gallery.

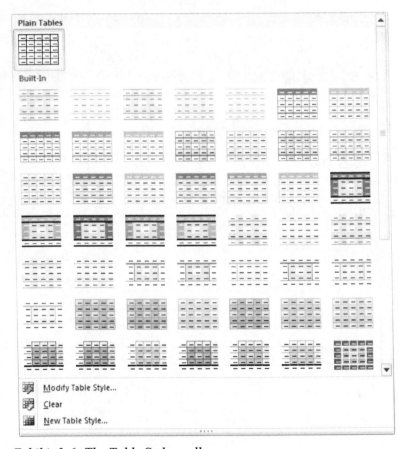

Exhibit 3-6: The Table Styles gallery

Do it!

D-1: Applying table styles

The files for this activity are in Student Data folder **Unit 3\Topic D**.

Here's how	Here's why
1 Open Quarterly sales2	
Save the document as **My quarterly sales2**	In the current topic folder.
2 Click any cell in the first table	
3 Click the **Design** tab	Under Table Tools.
4 In the Table Styles group, point to any table style	(Do not click the mouse button). As you point to each style, the document displays the resulting table format in the document window.
Click the style of your choice	To apply that style to the table.
5 Update the document	

Customizing table styles

Explanation
If the styles in the Table Styles gallery don't quite work for the data in your table, you can quickly select options that might correct the problem. For example, you might want to select a style because you like the shading and font; however, maybe you don't want the first column to be formatted differently from the rest of the table, which that style might do by default. In the Table Style Options group, you can select from several options for customizing a table style.

Do it!

D-2: Using table style options

Here's how	Here's why
1 Click in the first table	If necessary.
2 In the Table Styles group, click as shown	(The More button.) To expand the gallery.
In the gallery, select the Medium Shading 2 – Accent 4 style	(Use the ScreenTips to find this style.) Notice that this style formats each column differently. You want to use this style, but you don't want the last column formatted differently.
3 In the Table Style Options group, clear **Last Column**	
In the Table Style Options group, clear **Banded Rows**	
4 Update the document	

Using the Modify Style dialog box

Explanation

To customize a table style even further, you can use the Modify Style dialog box. Expand the Table Styles gallery and choose Modify Table Style to open the Modify Style dialog box, shown in Exhibit 3-7. The Modify Style dialog box for tables is similar to the one for text.

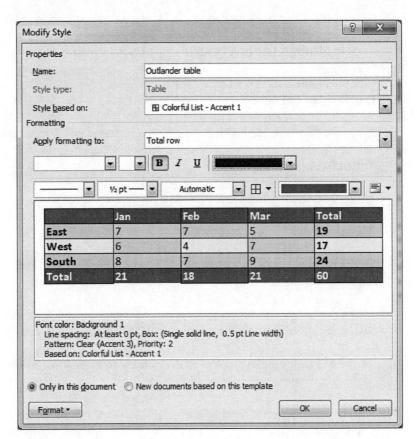

Exhibit 3-7: The Modify Style dialog box

Do it!   **D-3:   Modifying a table style**

Here's how	Here's why
1 Click in the second table	
2 Expand the Table Style gallery	In the Table Styles group, click the More button.
Choose **Modify Table Style...**	To open the Modify Style dialog box.
3 Edit the Name box to read **Outlander table**	
From the "Style based on" list, select **Colorful List – Accent 1**	You'll change the fill color and text color of the header row.
4 Under Formatting, from the "Apply formatting to" list, select **Header row**	
In the Fill Color gallery, select the dark green color	Olive Green, Accent 3, Darker 50%.
5 From the "Apply formatting to" list, select **Odd banded rows**	You'll apply a light green shade to the odd rows of the table.
In the Fill Color gallery, select the light green color	Olive Green, Accent 3, Lighter 60%.
6 Apply the dark green color to the fill for the Total row	(The bottom row of the table.) From the "Apply formatting" to list, select Total row. Select the dark green color (Olive Green, Accent 3, Darker 50%) from the Fill Color gallery.
In the Font Color gallery, select White, Background 1	
7 Click **OK**	To save the new style and apply it to the selected table.
8 Click any cell in the first table	
In the Table Styles group, click the **Outlander table** style	(It's now the first style in the gallery, under Custom.) To apply it to the first table. It looks slightly different because you selected options in the Table Style Options group earlier.
9 Update and close the document	

Unit summary: Formatting tables

Topic A   In this topic, you learned how to **align text** in a table, and you changed the orientation of text in a table cell. You also **merged** and **split** table cells, and you resized rows in a table.

Topic B   In this topic, you changed a table's **borders** and applied **shading** to table cells.

Topic C   In this topic, you used the Sort dialog box to **sort data** in a table. You also learned how to split a table and how to repeat a **header row** on multiple pages. Finally, you learned how to enter **formulas** in a table.

Topic D   In this topic, you applied and modified **table styles**.

Independent practice activity

In this activity, you'll format a table by aligning data in a column, applying a border, and shading selected cells. Then you'll sort the table data, insert a formula, and apply a table style.

The files for this activity are in Student Data folder **Unit 3\Unit summary**.

1 Open Table formatting practice and save it as **My table formatting practice**.

2 Align the data under the Earnings heading as **Align Text Right**.

3 To the header row (the row containing the column headings), apply a border that is a solid line, 1½ pt thick.

4 Shade the header row with a light blue color.

5 Sort the table by earnings, starting with the highest salary. (*Hint:* Remember to select all of the rows and columns, except the header row, before opening the Sort dialog box.)

6 Insert a new row at the bottom of the table.

7 In the rightmost cell of the last row, insert a formula that calculates the total of the salaries shown in the column. Adjust the column width, if necessary.

8 Apply a style of your choice from the Table Styles gallery to the table.

9 Split the table so that the row containing the column headers (Employee ID, Name, etc.) appears at the top of a table separate from the cells containing "Outlander Spices" and "Employee Information." (*Hint:* The employee data should all appear in one table, separate from the title, with the column headers in the top row. Delete any unnecessary rows from either table.)

10 Format the style of the second table (containing the employee data) to include a header row. (*Hint:* Check Header Row in the Table Style Options group.)

11 Format the table so that the header row is repeated on each page containing the table.

12 Update and close the document.

Review questions

1 What is the definition of merging cells?

2 You have a table that contains merged cells, and you want to add a new row in only one cell. How can you do this?

3 In the Sort dialog box, you have three options for how to sort data. One is alphabetically. What are the other two?

4 You have a table containing data that you want separated into two tables at a specific point. How can you do this?

5 Where can you find the setting for repeating the header row of a table?

6 You've applied a table style to a table, but the style formats the header row differently than the rest of the table. You want it formatted the same as the other rows. Where would you look to find settings to quickly adjust a table style?

7 You want to customize a table style beyond what is available in the Table Styles gallery. Where are the settings that you need to do this?

Unit 4

Printing labels and envelopes

Unit time: 30 minutes

Complete this unit, and you'll know how to:

A Prepare and print labels.

B Prepare and print envelopes.

Topic A: Labels

This topic covers the following Microsoft Office Specialist objectives for exam 77-887: Word Expert 2010.

#	Objective
4.3	**Create labels and forms**
	4.3.4 Create label forms

Explanation

After preparing a letter or package to send to an individual or organization, you'll need to create an address label. You can use Word's Envelopes and Labels dialog box to quickly prepare and print an address for an envelope or label of the size you specify.

Printing labels for a single recipient

To print a label by using the Envelopes and Labels dialog box:

1 Open or create a document.
2 Click the Mailings tab.
3 In the Create group, click Labels to open the Envelopes and Labels dialog box with the Labels tab active, as shown in Exhibit 4-1.
4 Click Options. Specify the printer and label information, and click OK.
5 Under Address (in the Envelopes and Labels dialog box), enter the address you want to print.
6 Click Print to print the document, or click New Document to generate a new document based on the settings you've specified. You can save the document to use as a label form in the future.

Exhibit 4-1: The Labels tab in the Envelopes and Labels dialog box

Inserting an address from Outlook

If you have address data stored in your Microsoft Outlook address book, you can insert it in the Envelopes and Labels dialog box. You can insert Outlook address data for an envelope or a label. To insert an address in the Envelopes and Labels dialog box:

1 Click the Insert Address button to open the Select Name dialog box.

2 Specify the contact address you want to add.

3 Click OK.

A-1:   Printing multiple labels for a single address

Here's how	Here's why
1 Create a new, blank document	Press Ctrl+N.
2 Click the **Mailings** tab	You often send packages to an associate in Phoenix, so you'll print a page of labels with her address on them.
In the Create group, click **Labels**	To open the Envelopes and Labels dialog box with the Labels tab active.
3 Click **Options**	To open the Label Options dialog box.
From the Label vendors list, select **Avery US Letter**	
From the Product number list, select **5160 Easy Peel Address Labels**	
Click **OK**	To close the Label Options dialog box and return to the Envelopes and Labels dialog box.
4 In the Address box, type **Southwestern Style Magazine**	
5 Press (↵ ENTER) and type **Attn: Christina Lanz**	
6 Press (↵ ENTER) and type **112 Rancho Blvd**	
7 Press (↵ ENTER) and type **Phoenix AZ 85005**	
8 Under Print, verify that **Full page of the same label** is selected	
Click **New Document**	To create a document with the label settings you selected.
9 If your computer is connected to a printer, press (CTRL) + (P)	
Click **Print**	To print the labels.
10 Save the document as **My labels**	In the current topic folder.
Close the document	

Topic B: Envelopes

This topic covers the following Microsoft Office Specialist objectives for exam 77-887: Word Expert 2010.

#	Objective
4.3	**Create labels and forms**
	4.3.3 Create envelope forms

Explanation

You can print single envelopes by using the Envelopes tab in the Envelopes and Labels dialog box. You can specify both the delivery and return addresses. If the current document is the letter you plan to send, then you might want to add the envelope as a page in the current document. In this way, you'll be able to print an envelope and the letter itself from the same document, and you won't need to use the Envelopes and Labels dialog box to generate the envelope in the future.

Printing an envelope for a single recipient

To print a single envelope:

1   Open or create a document.

2   Click the Mailings tab.

3   In the Create group, click Envelope to open the Envelopes and Labels dialog box with the Envelopes tab active, as shown in Exhibit 4-2.

4   Click Options to open the Envelope Options dialog box. Specify envelope and printing options, and click OK.

5   Under Delivery address and Return address (in the Envelopes and Labels dialog box), enter the appropriate addresses.

6   Click Print to print the document, or click New Document to generate a new document based on the settings you've specified. You can save the document to use as an envelope form in the future.

Exhibit 4-2: The Envelopes tab in the Envelopes and Labels dialog box

Do it!

B-1: Printing a single envelope

Here's how	Here's why
1 Create a new, blank document	If necessary.
2 On the Mailings tab, in the Create group, click **Envelopes**	To open the Envelopes and Labels dialog box with the Envelopes tab active.
3 Click **Options**	To open the Envelope Options dialog box.
4 In the Envelope size list, verify that **Size 10** is selected	
Click **OK**	To close the Envelope Options dialog box.
5 In the Delivery address box, type **Southwestern Style Magazine**	
6 Press (↵ ENTER)	
Type the following lines, pressing (↵ ENTER) after each line: **Attn: Christina Lanz** **112 Rancho Blvd** **Phoenix AZ 85005**	You won't enter a return address because you have envelopes with your return address printed on them.
7 Click **Add to Document**	To add the envelope as a page in the current document, where you can edit it.
8 If your computer is connected to a printer, press (CTRL) + (P) Click **Print**	
9 Save the document as **My envelope** Close the document	In the current topic folder.

Unit summary: Printing labels and envelopes

Topic A   In this topic, you used the Envelopes and Labels dialog box to prepare and print a sheet of **address labels**.

Topic B   In this topic, you used the Envelopes and Labels dialog box to prepare and print an address on a single **envelope**.

Independent practice activity

In this activity, you'll specify mailing addresses to print on a label and on an envelope.

1 Create a single mailing label that uses the 2163-Shipping label size.

2 For the label, specify the following address:
Daniel Hanson
Hanson Distributors
631 Industrial Pkwy
El Paso TX 79909

3 Specify that you will print a single label.

4 Print the label, or click Cancel.

5 Create an envelope that uses the following delivery address:
MK Franz
18 Franklin St
Frederick MD 21704

6 Specify the following return address:
Terry Park
Outlander Spices
28 Spice Way
Portland OR 97201

7 Verify that the addresses will print to a size 10 envelope. (*Hint:* Use the Envelope Options dialog box.)

8 Add the envelope to the current document. Do *not* save the return address as the default.

9 Save the file as **My practice envelope** in Student Data folder Unit 4\Unit summary.

10 Close all documents.

Review questions

1 In the Envelopes and Labels dialog box, how do you specify a label or envelope size?

2 After you create a label, what are the two printing choices available?

3 What is the advantage of adding an envelope to a document?

4 True or false? When you use the Envelopes and Labels dialog box to print addresses on envelopes, you must enter a return address.

Unit 5

Templates and building blocks

Unit time: 30 minutes

Complete this unit, and you'll know how to:

A Create a document from a template, save and use your own template, and use the Templates folder to store a custom template.

B Use the Building Blocks Organizer to work with commonly used document elements.

C Use the Restrict Formatting and Editing pane to protect a document with a password, and view and edit document properties.

Topic A: Template basics

This topic covers the following Microsoft Office Specialist objectives for exam 77-881: Word 2010.

#	Objective
1.6	**Apply a template to a document**
	1.6.1 Find templates
	1.6.1.1 Locate a template on your disk
	1.6.1.2 Find templates on the Web

This topic covers the following Microsoft Office Specialist objectives for exam 77-887: Word Expert 2010.

#	Objective
1.3	**Apply a template to a document**
	1.3.1 Modify an existing template
	1.3.2 Create a new template
	1.3.3 Apply a template to an existing document
	1.3.4 Manage templates by using the Organizer

Using templates to create documents

Explanation

Templates are documents that are specifically designed to be used as the basis for creating additional documents. Templates contain formatting and often contain boilerplate or placeholder text. By using templates for documents you create often— such as memos, faxes, and letters—you can save yourself a lot of time and effort and ensure consistency. Word 2010 templates have the .dotx file extension.

Word supplies many templates you can use to create documents. In fact, every time you create a document, you're using a template; Word bases new, blank documents on the Normal template. A new document's settings are all specified by the template settings. However, you can modify a template to change its default settings.

To use a template:

1 On the File tab, click New to display the Available Templates page. Word lists templates installed on your computer and those available on Office.com.

2 Click a category name to see the corresponding templates. For example, if you want to create a business form, click Forms and then click the Business folder.

3 Select the template you want to use. A preview will appear in the right-hand pane, as shown in Exhibit 5-1.

4 Click Create to use a template that's stored locally, or click Download to use an online template.

When you create a document from a template, you don't actually edit the original template. Instead, Word creates a copy of it, but with the .docx extension.

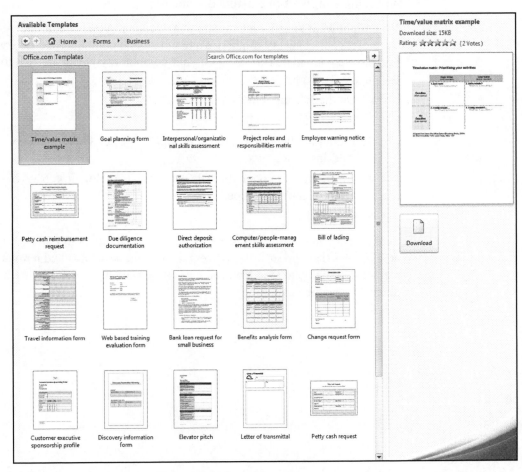

Exhibit 5-1: The Business Forms template category

Applying templates to existing documents

You might want to apply a template to a document you have already created. For example, your company might use a template that contains specific styles and macros. If you have the template file saved on your computer, you can apply it to an open document. To do so:

1   On the File tab, click Options.

2   Click Add-Ins.

3   From the Manage list, select Templates. Click Go to open the Templates and Add-ins dialog box.

4   Click Attach to open the Attach Template dialog box. Navigate to the template, select it, and click Open.

5   Click OK.

In the Templates and Add-ins dialog box, you can click Organizer to examine the styles and macros that appear in the current document, in its attached template, and in the default Normal template. You can copy styles and macros from one to the other, delete them, or rename them.

Do it!   **A-1:   Using a template**

Here's how	Here's why
1 On the File tab, click **New**	To display the Available Templates page.
2 Click **Sample templates**	To see some of the templates installed on the computer.
Click ⌂ Home	To go back to the main Available Templates page. You'll search for the kind of template you're looking for.
3 In the "Search Office.com for templates" box, type **memo**	

Available Templates

⬅ ➡ ⌂ Home ▸ More categories

Office.com Templates | memo | ➡

Press ⏎ ENTER	Word displays the search results.
Select **Memo (Simple design)**	If necessary.
Click **Download**	To create a document from the selected template. Word provides fields that contain prompts for information for the memo.
Close the Document Information panel	If necessary.
4 Save the document as **My memo**	(In Student Data folder Unit 5\Topic A.) A message box asks whether you want to save the document in the new file format.
Click **OK**	
5 Click the indicated field	

Company

[Company·name]

Type **Outlander Spices**	
Press TAB twice	To go to the Author field.
Type **Ann Salinski**	
6 Update and close the document	

Creating templates

Explanation

You can save a document as a template, so you can create templates that include the text, graphics, tables, and objects of your choice. When you save a file as a template, it's saved in the .dotx file format.

To save a document as a template:

1 Open a document, create a new blank document, or create a document from a template.
2 Enter or edit text as needed, and apply the formatting you want the template to contain.
3 Insert any tables, objects, or pictures that you want the template to contain.
4 On the File tab, click Save As.
5 From the Save as type list, select Word Template.
6 In the File name box, enter a name for the template.
7 Click Save.

Do it!

A-2: Saving an altered template

Here's how	Here's why
1 On the File tab, click **New**	
2 Click **Faxes**	To see the fax templates at Office.com.
From the list of templates, select **Fax cover sheet (Contemporary design)**	You'll enter information on the cover sheet and save the altered document as a new template.
Click **Download**	
3 In the top-left corner of the document, click the **Address** field	You don't want to have to type the address each time you use this template.
Type **1150 Grant St., San Francisco, CA 94113**	
4 On the File tab, click **Save As**	To open the Save As dialog box.
5 In the File name box, type **My template**	
From the Save as type list, select **Word Template**	
Navigate to the current topic folder, and click **Save**	(Student Data folder Unit 5\Topic A.) A message box asks whether you want to save the document in the new file format.
Click **OK**	
6 Close the document	

Using your own templates

Explanation

After you've created a template, you can create a document from it, just as you would with one of Word's built-in templates. To use your own templates (if they're not stored in Word's Templates folder):

1 On the File tab, click New.

2 Click "New from existing."

3 Locate and select the template you want to use.

4 Click Create New.

Do it!

A-3: Creating a document from a user-defined template

The files for this activity are in Student Data folder **Unit 5\Topic A**.

Here's how	Here's why
1 On the File tab, click **New**	
2 Click **New from existing**	To open the New from Existing Document dialog box.
3 Navigate to the current topic folder	If necessary.
Select **Outlander fax template**	
Click **Create New**	To create a document based on this template. Notice that the new document is given a generic file name, rather than the name of the template.
4 Close the document	

Using the Templates folder

Explanation

If you create your own templates and plan to use them frequently, it's a good idea to store them in Word's Templates folder. That way, you won't have to search for them whenever you want to use them.

To use a custom template that you've stored in Word's Templates folder:

1 On the File tab, click New.
2 Click My templates to open the New dialog box, shown in Exhibit 5-2.
3 Select the template you want to use.
4 Click OK.

To save a template in Word's Templates folder, navigate to the folder's default location, which is C:\Users\\[*user name*\]\AppData\Roaming\Microsoft\Templates. A shortcut to this folder is available in the top-left corner of the Save As dialog box.

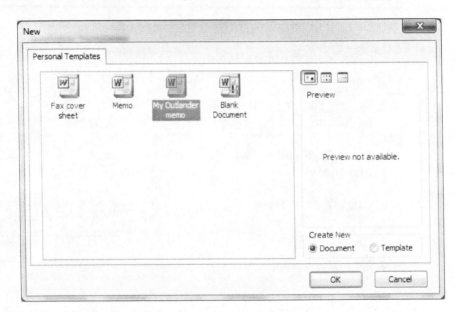

Exhibit 5-2: The New dialog box

Do it!

A-4: Saving a template in the Templates folder

The files for this activity are in Student Data folder **Unit 5\Topic A**.

Here's how	Here's why
1 Open Outlander memo	You will save this document as a template in the Templates folder so that it will be readily available whenever you use Microsoft Word.
2 On the File tab, click **Save As**	
From the Save as type list, select **Word Template**	
Edit the File name box to read **My Outlander memo**	
3 On the left side of the Save As dialog box, click the arrow next to Microsoft Word	
	(Scroll up to see the item.) To show the Templates folder, if necessary.
Click **Templates**	To select the folder.
Click **Save**	
4 Close the document	
5 On the File tab, click **New**	
Click **My templates**	
Select **My Outlander memo**	
Click **OK**	To create a document based on the My Outlander memo template.
6 Close the document	

Topic B: Building blocks

This topic covers the following Microsoft Office Specialist objectives for exam 77-887: Word Expert 2010.

#	Objective
2.3	**Construct reusable content in a document**
	2.3.1 Create customized building blocks
	2.3.2 Save a selection as a Quick Part
	2.3.3 Save Quick Parts after a document is saved
3.3	**Construct content in a document by using the Quick Parts tool**
	3.3.1 Add built-in building blocks
	3.3.1.2 Text boxes
	3.3.1.3 Header
	3.3.1.7 Equations
3.5	**Create and modify headers and footers**
	3.5.5 Add content to a header or footer
	3.5.5.1 Custom dialog box
4.4	**Apply and manipulate text boxes**
	4.4.2 Save a selection to the Text Box gallery
	4.4.6 Apply 3-D effects

Adding content with building blocks

Explanation

A *building block* is a predefined portion of content—such as a cover page, header, or footer—that can be reused. Word provides a set of commonly used building blocks, organized in galleries on the Ribbon. For example, the Cover Page gallery, on the Insert tab, contains all the cover-page building blocks. When you select a cover page from the gallery, it's already formatted with a certain look. It's automatically placed at the beginning of your document, and it contains placeholders, such as "[Type the document title]," indicating where you can enter your text. By using building blocks, you can create documents much more quickly.

Using the Building Blocks Organizer

Building blocks provide a cohesive look for your documents. For example, the Cover Page, Header, and Footer galleries each contain a building block named Alphabet. Each one incorporates the same color scheme and fonts, among other attributes. By using all three of these building blocks, you create a document with a cover page, headers, and footers that all use a consistent style.

You can insert building blocks by selecting them from individual galleries, or you can access all building blocks, from all galleries, in the Building Blocks Organizer, shown in Exhibit 5-3.

To open the Building Blocks Organizer:

1   Click the Insert tab.

2   In the Text group, click Quick Parts and choose Building Blocks Organizer.

Each building block is associated with a name, gallery, category, template, behavior, and description. To find a building block more quickly, you can sort the list displayed in the Building Block Organizer. To do so, click the heading of the column by which you want to sort.

For example, if you know the name of the building block you want to use, click the Name column heading to sort alphabetically by building block name. Or if you know you'd like a cover page, but you're not sure which style, click the Gallery column heading to see all of the cover-page building blocks arranged together.

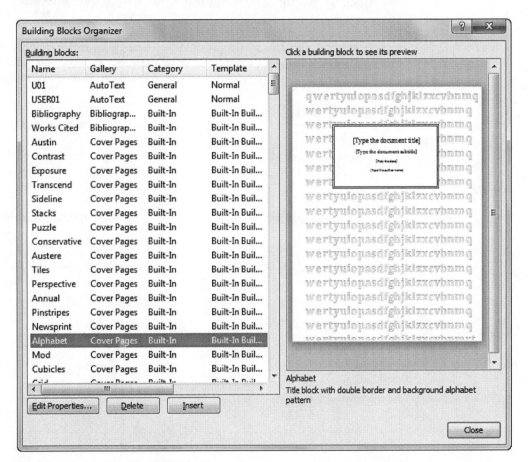

Exhibit 5-3: The Building Blocks Organizer

Inserting equations

One kind of building block that could be particularly useful is the equation building block, because equations can be very difficult to format correctly and often contain a number of special characters. To insert an equation in a document, click the Insert tab, click Equation, and select the equation building block you want to insert.

Do it!

B-1: Using the Building Blocks Organizer

Here's how	Here's why
1 Create a new blank document	You'll observe the Building Blocks Organizer.
2 Click the **Insert** tab	
In the Text group, click **Quick Parts** and choose **Building Blocks Organizer...**	To open the Building Blocks Organizer dialog box.
3 Click the **Name** column heading	To sort the list alphabetically by building block name.
4 In the Building blocks list, locate the Alphabet building blocks	There are several building blocks with this name, but each one is a different document component, located in a different gallery.
Observe the Gallery column	There are Alphabet building blocks in the Footers, Cover Pages, and Headers galleries.
Select **Alphabet**	(From any gallery.) Notice the preview displayed on the right. Below the preview is a description of the document element.
5 Click the **Gallery** column heading	To sort the building blocks by gallery name.
Scroll the building block list	There are galleries of bibliographies, cover pages, equations, footers, headers, page numbers, and more.

Adding a building block to a document

Explanation

The Building Block Organizer lists many building blocks. In addition to cover pages, headers, and footers, there are also sidebars. A *sidebar* is a formatted text box that appears along the side of a document page.

To insert a building block in a document:

1 Click the Insert tab.
2 In the Text group, click Quick Parts and choose Building Blocks Organizer.
3 From the Building blocks list, select the desired building block.
4 Click Insert.

Content controls

Many building blocks contain placeholders, called *content controls*, that you can customize with your information. To do so, click the placeholder and begin typing.

Do it!

B-2: Inserting building blocks

Here's how	Here's why
1 In the Building Blocks Organizer, click the **Name** column heading	To sort building blocks by name.
2 From the Building blocks list, select **Annual Sidebar**	
Click **Insert**	To add this building block to the document. The Drawing Tools | Format tab appears.
3 Save the document as **My report**	In Student Data folder Unit 5\Topic B.
4 In the Shape Styles group, click **Shape Effects** and point to **3-D Rotation**	To display a gallery of three-dimensional effects that can be applied to the shape.
Under Perspective, select Perspective Right, as shown	
5 In the Arrange group, click **Position**	
Under With Text Wrapping, select the indicated option	
	(Position in Top Left with Square Text Wrapping.) To position the sidebar on the left side of the page.
6 Open the Building Blocks Organizer	On the Insert tab, click Quick Parts and choose Building Blocks Organizer.
Press ⓟ	To move to the building blocks with names beginning with the letter P. You want to select a header named Pinstripes.
From the Headers gallery, select **Pinstripes**	
Click **Insert**	

7	In the header, click **Type the document title**	(If necessary.) To select the content control.
	Type **Company Report**	: Title Company Report
8	Update the document	

Creating your own building blocks

Explanation

You might want to create your own building blocks and store them in the Building Blocks Organizer. For example, if you have a company logo and contact information that you'll often need to include in documents, you can store them as building blocks. That way, you won't have to re-create these elements each time you want to use them.

To create your own building block:

1 In your document, select the element (such as a company logo or address) that you want to save as a building block.

2 On the Insert tab, in the Text group, click Quick Parts and choose Save Selection to Quick Part Gallery. This opens the Create New Building Block dialog box, shown in Exhibit 5-4.

3 In the Name box, enter a name for the building block.

4 From the Gallery list, select the gallery in which you want to store the building block. For example, you might want to save a text box in the Text Boxes gallery.

5 From the Category list, select a category for the building block. If you want to add a new category, select Create New Category from the list.

6 In the Description box, enter information about the building block.

7 From the Save in list, select the template in which you want to save the building block.

8 From the Options list, specify whether to include content only or to include breaks to place content in its own paragraph or on its own page.

9 Click OK.

Exhibit 5-4: The Create New Building Block dialog box

Building block properties

You can modify the properties of custom and built-in building blocks in the Building Blocks Organizer. For example, you can change a building block's name, assign it to a different gallery or category, edit its description, and specify how it's inserted in a document. To do so, open the Building Blocks Organizer, select the building block you want to change, and click Edit Properties to open the Modify Building Block dialog box.

Do it!

B-3: Creating building blocks

The files for this activity are in Student Data folder **Unit 5\Topic B**.

Here's how	Here's why
1 Open Building blocks	
2 Click the Outlander Spices logo	(At the top of the page.) To select this graphic element. You'll save this as a building block so that it can easily be used in other documents.
3 On the Insert tab, in the Text group, click **Quick Parts** and choose **Save Selection to Quick Part Gallery...**	To open the Create New Building Block dialog box.
Edit the Name box to read **Outlander graphic**	To name the building block.
From the Options list, select **Insert content in its own paragraph**	You'll use the defaults for the other options.
Click **OK**	To save this graphic element as a building block.
4 Select the company contact information, as shown	1150 Grant Street San Francisco, CA 94113 Phone: (415) 969-9900 Fax: (415) 969-9909
	You'll save this as a building block as well.
5 In the Text group, click **Quick Parts** and choose **Save Selection to Quick Part Gallery...**	
Edit the Name box to read **Outlander contact info**	
From the Gallery list, select **Text Boxes**	To specify that this text box will appear in the Text Boxes gallery.
From the Options list, select **Insert content in its own paragraph**	
Click **OK**	
6 Close the Building blocks document	

7	In the My report document, close the header	
	Place the insertion point in the blank area of the document	To move it out of the sidebar, if necessary.
8	Open the Building Blocks Organizer	
	Move to the building blocks with names beginning with "O"	Press O.
	Select **Outlander graphic**	
	Click **Insert**	To add the Outlander graphic to the report.
9	Press ⏎ ENTER	To create a new line in the report. Next, you'll add the contact information building block.

Altering building blocks

Explanation

After you create a building block, you might want to modify it. For example, perhaps your company logo or address needs to be updated. To modify a building block:

1 In your document, select the updated building block.
2 On the Insert tab, click Quick Parts and choose Save Selection to Quick Part Gallery to open the Create New Building Block dialog box.
3 In the Name box, enter the name you previously used for the building block.
4 Specify the remaining options in the dialog box as desired.
5 Click OK. A message box asks if you want to redefine the previous building block entry.
6 Click Yes to replace the previous building block with the updated one.

Removing a building block

If a building block becomes obsolete, you can remove it. To delete a building block:

1 Open the Building Blocks Organizer.
2 From the Building blocks list, select the building block you want to delete.
3 Click Delete.
4 Click Yes to confirm the deletion.
5 Click Close to close the Building Blocks Organizer.

Saving changes to building blocks

After you've been working with and modifying building blocks and you close Word, a warning box will appear, asking whether you want to save the modifications you've made, as shown in Exhibit 5-5. To do so, click Save.

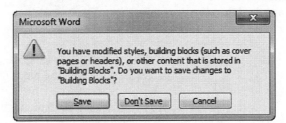

Exhibit 5-5: Saving changes to "Building Blocks"

Do it!

B-4: Modifying a building block

Here's how	Here's why
1 Add the **Outlander contact info** building block to the My report document, below the logo	Open the Building Blocks Organizer, select Outlander contact info, and click Insert.
2 Edit the street address to read **1150 Main Street**	
3 Select the company contact information	1150 Main Street San Francisco, CA 94113 Phone: (415) 969-9900 Fax: (415) 969-9909
4 In the Text group, click **Quick Parts** and choose **Save Selection to Quick Part Gallery...**	On the Insert tab.
Edit the Name box to read **Outlander contact info**	This is the same name you originally used to save this building block.
From the Gallery list, select **Text Boxes**	
From the Options list, select **Insert content in its own paragraph**	
Click **OK**	A message box appears, asking if you want to redefine the building block entry.
Click **Yes**	To replace the old building block with this updated version.
5 Update and close the document	

Topic C: Document properties

This topic covers the following Microsoft Office Specialist objectives for exam 77-881: Word 2010.

#	Objective
1.2	**Apply protection to a document**
	1.2.1 Apply protection by using the Microsoft Office Backstage view commands
	1.2.1.1 Apply controls and restrictions to document access
	1.2.1.2 Password-protect a document
	1.2.2 Applying protection by using the Ribbon commands

This topic covers the following Microsoft Office Specialist objectives for exam 77-887: Word Expert 2010.

#	Objective
1.2	**Apply protection to a document**
	1.2.1 Restrict editing
	1.2.2 Apply controls or restrictions to document access

Protecting documents

Explanation

After you've created a document, you might want to protect it so that other users can't change something without authorization. You can assign a password to the document to protect it, and you can specify which kinds of changes you will allow people to make. In addition, you can view and edit document properties. These provide more information and can provide added security.

You can protect documents by setting editing and formatting restrictions and by assigning passwords to them. Two types of restrictions can be assigned:

- *Formatting restrictions* prevent someone from modifying or using styles that you specify. This can effectively prevent other people from applying any formatting to a document.

- *Editing restrictions* let you select the kind of editing allowed in a document: Tracked Changes, Comments, Filling in forms, or No changes (Read only).

To specify formatting and editing restrictions:

1   Click the File tab. On the Info page, click the Protect Document button and choose Restrict Editing to open the Restrict Formatting and Editing pane, shown in Exhibit 5-6.

2   Under Formatting restrictions, check the box to limit formatting to a selection of styles. Then click Settings to open the Formatting Restrictions dialog box. Select the desired options and click OK.

3   Under Editing restrictions, check the box to apply editing restrictions; then select an option from the list.

4   Under Start Enforcement, click "Yes, Start Enforcing Protection" to open the Start Enforcing Protection dialog box.

5   Enter a password; then reenter it to confirm it.

6   Click OK.

You can also open the Restrict Formatting and Editing pane by clicking the Review tab and then clicking Restrict Editing in the Protect group.

After a document is protected, you can remove protection by clicking Stop Protection in the Restrict Formatting and Editing pane. When you do, the Unprotect Document dialog box will open, and you can enter the password.

Exhibit 5-6: The Restrict Formatting and Editing pane

You can also protect a document with a password without specifying formatting and editing restrictions. To do so, click File; on the Info page, click the Protect Document button and choose Encrypt with Password. In the Encrypt Document dialog box, enter the desired password and click OK. When you're prompted to re-enter the password, do so and click OK again.

Once a document is password-protected, it can be opened only by entering the password. To remove password protection, click the Protect Document button on the Info page and choose Encrypt with Password. In the Encrypt Document dialog box, clear the Password box and click OK.

Password guidelines

When creating passwords, follow these guidelines:

- Passwords are case sensitive.
- Passwords can contain up to 15 characters.
- Any combination of letters, numerals, spaces, and symbols can be used.
- Including capital letters and numbers creates stronger passwords.
- Be sure to remember the password. Lost passwords cannot be recovered.

Do it!

C-1: Protecting a document

The files for this activity are in Student Data folder **Unit 5\Topic C**.

Here's how	Here's why
1 Open Spice info	
Save the document as **My spice info**	In the current topic folder.
2 Click the **File** tab	
Click **Protect Document** and choose **Restrict Editing**	To open the Restrict Formatting and Editing pane.
3 Under Editing restrictions, check the checkbox	You will leave the list set to "No changes (Read only)" to make the document read-only.
Under Start enforcement, click **Yes, Start Enforcing Protection**	To open the Start Enforcing Protection dialog box.
4 In the "Enter new password (optional)" box, type **password1**	
In the "Reenter password to confirm" box, type **password1**	
Click **OK**	To close the dialog box.
5 Try to edit the document	You can't, because the document is read-only. In the Restrict Formatting and Editing pane, a message indicates the document permissions.
6 In the Restrict Formatting and Editing pane, click **Stop Protection**	(At the bottom of the pane.) To open the Unprotect Document dialog box.
In the Password box, type **password1** and click **OK**	You can now edit the document.
7 Close the Restrict Formatting and Editing pane	

8 Click the **File** tab	You'll protect the document so that it can be opened only by entering a password.
Click **Protect Document** and choose **Encrypt with Password**	To open the Encrypt Document dialog box.
In the Password box, type **password2**	
Click **OK**	You're prompted to reenter the password.
Type **password2** and click **OK**	To protect the document.
9 Update and close the document, then reopen it	The Password dialog box appears.
Type **password2** and click **OK**	To open the document.
10 On the Info page, click **Protect Document** and choose **Encrypt with Password**	
Clear the Password box and click **OK**	To remove the password protection.
11 Update the document	

Editing document properties

Explanation

Each Word document file stores information about the document itself. A document's properties are also referred to as *metadata*. To view and edit the properties of the active document:

1 Click the File tab.

2 Click Info (if it's not already selected).

3 On the right side of the Info page, click Properties and choose Show Document Panel.

The Document Panel, shown in Exhibit 5-7, appears above the current document. The panel provides a variety of information about the document or template. Enter information in the boxes to save that information as part of the document. You can then easily organize and identify your documents later based on this information.

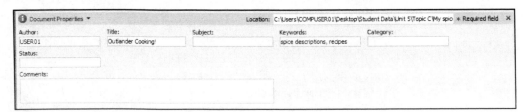

Exhibit 5-7: The Document Panel

Do it!

C-2:   Viewing and editing document properties

Here's how	Here's why
1 Click the **File** tab and then click **Info**	(If necessary.) To display information about the current document and its properties.
2 Under Properties, in the Title box, type **Outlander Cooking!**	Properties ▾ Size — 138KB Pages — 17 Words — 3241 Total Editing Time — 0 Minutes Title — Outlander Cooking!
3 In the Tags box, type **spice descriptions, recipes**	
4 Click **Properties** and choose **Show Document Panel**	To open the Document Panel above the current document. The properties you entered appear in the panel.
5 Update the document	

Document statistics

Explanation

To quickly display some statistics about a document, click the word count area on the left side of the status bar. This opens the Word Count dialog box, shown in Exhibit 5-8. The dialog box shows information about the text in the document.

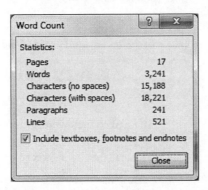

Exhibit 5-8: Document statistics

To view more statistics about the document, including the date it was created and modified, open the <Document> Properties dialog box, shown in Exhibit 5-9. To do so, first open the Document Panel. Then, from the Document Properties list (in the upper-left corner of the Document Panel), choose Advanced Properties.

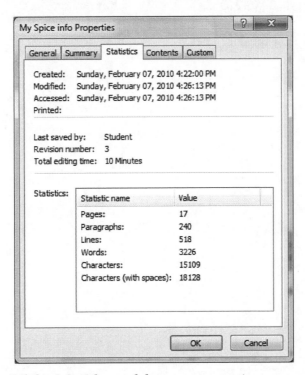

Exhibit 5-9: Advanced document properties

Do it!

C-3:   Viewing document statistics

Here's how	Here's why
1 In the Document Panel, click as shown	ⓘ Document Properties ▼ Author: In the upper-left corner of the panel.
Choose **Advanced Properties...**	To open the Properties dialog box for the current document.
2 Click the **Statistics** tab	To display document statistics.
Click **OK**	To close the dialog box.
3 On the left side of the status bar, click the word count area, as shown	Words: 3,241 To open the Word Count dialog box, which displays some document properties.
Click **Close**	To close the dialog box.
4 Close the Document Panel	
5 Update and close the document	

Unit summary: Templates and building blocks

Topic A   In this topic, you learned how to create a document from a **template**. Then you saved and used your own template, and you learned how to use the Templates folder to store a custom template.

Topic B   In this topic, you used the **Building Blocks Organizer** to insert a sidebar and a header into a document. You also created your own building blocks for a company graphic and contact information, and you learned how to modify building blocks.

Topic C   In this topic, you used the Restrict Formatting and Editing pane to **protect** a document with a password. Then you viewed and edited document **properties**. You also learned how to display a document's statistics.

Independent practice activity

In this activity, you'll create a document from a template. Then you'll edit the document and save it as a new template in Word's Templates folder. Next, you'll enable password protection for a document and edit its properties.

The files for this activity are in Student Data folder **Unit 5\Unit summary**.

1 Create a document from the Office.com Meeting minutes template. (*Hint:* Search for the template. Use one of the templates provided by Microsoft, as indicated above the preview of the template.)

2 Edit the Presenter field so that it displays your name.

3 Save the document as a template named **My practice minutes** in Word's Templates folder. (*Hint:* Use the Save As dialog box to navigate to the Templates folder.)

4 Close the document.

5 Open Practice properties, and save it as **My practice properties** (in Student Data folder Unit 5\Unit summary).

6 Protect the document so that no changes are allowed without the password **password**.

7 Show the document properties.

8 In the Author field, enter your name.

9 Display the statistics for the document.

10 Close the document properties and the Restrict Formatting and Editing pane.

11 Update and close the document.

Review questions

1 When you create a Word document, which template is used by default?

2 What are the steps for creating a document based on a template?

3 Where should you save a template you've created or customized so that it is easily accessible?

4 Which of the following statements about building blocks is false?

A Examples of building blocks include predefined headers, footers, and cover pages.

B To open the Building Blocks Organizer, click the Insert tab; then, in the Text group, click Building Blocks Organizer.

C A building block is a predefined portion of content.

D Building blocks can provide a cohesive look for your documents.

5 Where can you set a password to protect a document from unwanted edits?

A The Restrict Formatting and Editing pane

B The Properties pane

C The Application Settings dialog box

D The Password group

6 The Word Count dialog box shows all of the following information about a document, except:

A Pages

B Words

C Paragraphs

D Author

Unit 6

Graphics

Unit time: 45 minutes

Complete this unit, and you'll know how to:

A Create and modify a diagram.

B Insert text boxes and shapes in a document, and adjust their size, shape, and other attributes.

C Format text graphically, using WordArt, drop caps, and pull quotes.

Topic A: Creating diagrams

This topic covers the following Microsoft Office Specialist objectives for exam 77-881: Word 2010.

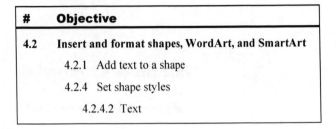

#	Objective
4.2	**Insert and format shapes, WordArt, and SmartArt**
	4.2.1 Add text to a shape
	4.2.4 Set shape styles
	4.2.4.2 Text

Using SmartArt graphics

Explanation

You can use Word to create diagrams, such as organization charts, that visually represent relationships or processes. You can insert a diagram by using the Choose a SmartArt Graphic dialog box, shown in Exhibit 6-1. You can choose from some commonly used standard diagrams, such as process, cycle, or hierarchy diagrams.

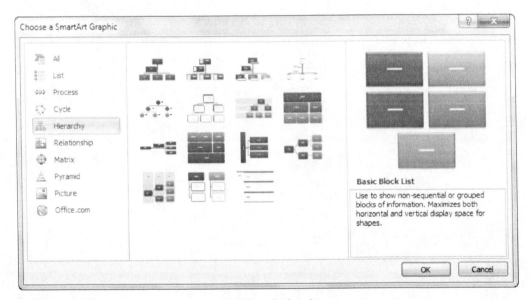

Exhibit 6-1: The Choose a SmartArt Graphic dialog box

To insert a diagram into a document:

1   Place the insertion point where you want to insert the diagram.

2   Click the Insert tab.

3   In the Illustrations group, click SmartArt to open the Choose a SmartArt Graphic dialog box.

4   On the left, select a diagram type.

5   From the list of diagrams in that category, select the specific diagram you want.

6   Click OK to insert the diagram on a *drawing canvas* (the space in which you work on graphics or drawings). The Text pane appears, containing the diagram's placeholder text.

7   Click a text placeholder, and type the text you want to display in the diagram.

When you insert or work with SmartArt graphics, Word displays the SmartArt Tools | Design and SmartArt Tools | Format tabs.

Adding text to a SmartArt graphic

After your SmartArt graphic is inserted in a document, you can add text to it by using the Text pane. To show this pane, select the SmartArt graphic. Then, on the SmartArt Tools | Design tab, in the Create Graphic group, click Text Pane. (You can also click the control icon on the left edge of the frame that appears around the graphic when it's selected.) To hide this pane, click Text Pane again.

Do it!

A-1: Creating an organization chart

Here's how	Here's why
1 Create a new, blank document	
Save the document as **My org chart1**	In Student Data folder Unit 6\Topic A.
2 Click the **Insert** tab	
In the Illustrations group, click **SmartArt**	To open the Choose a SmartArt Graphic dialog box.
3 On the left, select **Hierarchy**	To select the Hierarchy category of graphics.
Click	(The Hierarchy option.) To select the type of chart you'd like to create.
Click **OK**	To insert the organization chart on the page. The Text pane for the graphic opens.
4 In the Text pane, under "Type your text here," click the first bullet	(If necessary.) To select it so you can enter custom text.
Type **VP Global Sales**	The text appears in the top box of the chart.
5 Click the second bullet point	(In the Text pane.) This bullet is subordinate to the first, so the box is located in the second row of the chart, with a connecting line between the two boxes.
Type **Director North American Sales**	As you type, Word automatically aligns and sizes the text within the box.
6 Press ⏎ ENTER	To create another bullet point at the same level as the previous one. A new box is created on the second row.
Type **Director Global Sales**	
7 Press ⏎ ENTER	
Press TAB	To demote the bullet point to the third level.
Type **Director European Sales**	

8 Press (↵ ENTER) and type
   Director Pacific Rim Sales

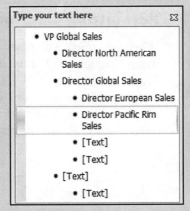

To create another third-level bullet point. Now
you'll remove the bullet points you don't need.

9 Point to the [Text] bullet below
   the one you just added

   Drag down to select the remaining
   [Text] bullet points

   Press (← BACKSPACE)

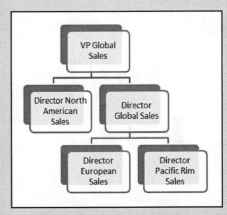

To remove the extra boxes from the chart.

10 In the Create Graphic group, click
   Text Pane

   (On the SmartArt Tools | Design tab.) To close
   the Text pane.

11 Update the document

Formatting diagrams

Explanation

When you select a diagram, a border appears around it, and Word adds the SmartArt Tools | Design and Format tabs to the Ribbon. You can use these tabs to change the layout and formatting of your diagram. Use the SmartArt Tools | Design tab to change the diagram type or layout, change the diagram shapes, and apply Quick Styles to the diagram. Use the SmartArt Tools | Format tab to modify and format individual diagram shapes and to format the diagram text.

Do it!   **A-2:   Formatting an organization chart**

Here's how	Here's why
1 Verify that the organization chart is selected	A frame appears around the chart when it is selected.
2 On the SmartArt Tools | Design tab, in the SmartArt Styles group, click **Change Colors**	To display a color gallery.
Under Colorful, select the first option	(Colorful - Accent Colors.) To apply the color scheme to the chart.
3 In the SmartArt Styles group, click the More button	To display the SmartArt Styles gallery.
Under 3-D, select Inset, as shown	
	To apply the 3-D Inset style to the chart. Next, you'll format individual objects.
4 Click the **Format** tab	(Under SmartArt Tools.) You'll format the second-level shapes to use a different color.
5 Click the boundary of the indicated shape	
	To select the shape containing "Director North American Sales."
Press CTRL and click the shape containing "Director Global Sales"	To select both shapes.
6 In the Shape Styles group, click the **Shape Fill** arrow	To open the Shape Fill gallery.
Select the light blue color	Blue, Accent 1, Lighter 80%.
7 Update and close the document	

Topic B: Using the Drawing tools

This topic covers the following Microsoft Office Specialist objectives for exam 77-881: Word 2010.

#	Objective
4.1	**Insert and format pictures in a document**
	4.1.5 Modify a shape
4.2	**Insert and format shapes, WordArt, and SmartArt**
	4.2.1 Add text to a shape
	4.2.2 Modify text on a shape
	4.2.4 Set shape styles
	4.2.4.1 Border
	4.2.5 Adjust position and size
4.4	**Apply and manipulate text boxes**
	4.4.1 Format text boxes
	4.4.3 Apply text box styles
	4.4.4 Change text direction
	4.4.5 Apply shadow effects

This topic covers the following Microsoft Office Specialist objectives for exam 77-887: Word Expert 2010.

#	Objective
2.4	**Link sections**
	2.4.1 Link text boxes
	2.4.2 Break links between text boxes

Drawing shapes

Explanation

You can add a variety of shapes to a Word document. You can add basic geometric shapes and symbols, lines, block arrows, flowchart symbols, callouts, stars, and banners.

You can draw shapes by selecting a shape from the Shapes gallery. To open the Shapes gallery, click the Insert tab and then click Shapes in the Illustrations group. After selecting a shape, you can drag to draw it in the document. If you press Shift while drawing a shape, it will maintain its original proportions.

When you create or work with shapes, Word displays the Drawing Tools | Format tab on the Ribbon.

Do it!

B-1: Drawing a shape

The files for this activity are in Student Data folder **Unit 6\Topic B**.

Here's how	Here's why
1 Open Org chart2	
Save the document as **My org chart2**	In the current topic folder.
2 Click the chart	(If necessary.) To select it.
3 On the Insert tab, in the Illustrations group, click **Shapes**	To open the Shapes gallery.
Under Block Arrows, select the first arrow, as shown	
4 Position the pointer as shown	
Drag to the right, as shown	
	To create an arrow.
5 Update the document	

Modifying shapes

Explanation

After creating a shape, you can modify it in a variety of ways. You can move, resize, reshape, or rotate it. In addition, you can specify a shape's fill and line attributes.

Moving a shape

When you point inside a shape or along its edge, the pointer appears with a four-headed arrow at its tip, as shown in Exhibit 6-2. This pointer indicates that you can drag to move the shape. In addition, after you select a shape, you can press the arrow keys to nudge the shape in small increments for precise positioning.

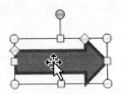

Exhibit 6-2: The pointer as it appears when placed within a shape

Resizing a shape

When you select a shape, *sizing handles* appear at each corner and along each edge of the shape's boundary. When you point to a sizing handle, the pointer appears as a two-headed arrow, as shown in Exhibit 6-3. Dragging a sizing handle resizes the shape:

- Drag a sizing handle along an edge to change only the height or only the width.
- Drag a corner sizing handle to change the width and height.
- Press Shift while dragging a corner sizing handle to change the width and height proportionally.

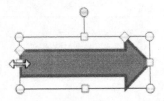

Exhibit 6-3: The pointer as it appears when placed on a sizing handle

Rotating a shape

When you select a shape, a green *rotate handle* appears above it. When you point to the rotate handle, the pointer appears as a circular arrow, as shown in Exhibit 6-4. You can drag the rotate handle to rotate the shape.

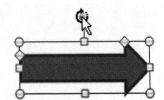

Exhibit 6-4: The pointer as it appears when placed on a rotate handle

Reshaping a shape

When you select a shape, it might display a yellow *adjustment handle*. You can drag an adjustment handle to reshape the shape. For example, with an arrow shape, you can change the thickness and length of the line part, change the size or shape of the arrowhead, or make the whole arrow short and thick or long and thin—to name just a few variations. When you point to an adjustment handle, the pointer appears as a white arrowhead, as shown in Exhibit 6-5.

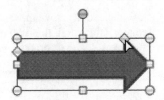

Exhibit 6-5: The pointer as it appears when placed on an adjustment handle

Adding text to a shape

To enter text within a shape, right-click inside the shape and choose Add Text. Then type the desired text.

Do it!   **B-2:   Modifying a shape**

Here's how	Here's why
1 Point to the arrow shape	 A four-headed arrow appears at the tip of the pointer, indicating that you can click to select the arrow shape or drag to move it.
Drag the arrow to position it as shown	
2 Point to the left-center sizing handle, as shown	 The pointer appears as a two-headed horizontal arrow, indicating that you can drag to change the shape's width.
Drag to the right	 To shorten the arrow shape.
3 On the Insert tab, in the Illustrations group, click **Shapes**	
Under Stars and Banners, select the Wave shape, as shown	
In the upper-right corner of the document, drag to create the wave shape	
4 Right-click inside the shape	To display a shortcut menu.
Choose **Add Text**	
Type **Outlander Spices**	

5 Press CTRL + A	To select the text.
Format the text as Trebuchet MS, 24 pt, bold, centered	
Resize the shape	If necessary, to accommodate the text.
6 Update the document	

Using text boxes

Explanation

Text boxes are drawn objects in which you can enter text. You can arrange text boxes independently of other text or objects in the document area. To draw a text box:

1   Click the Insert tab.
2   In the Text group, click Text Box and choose Draw Text Box. The pointer changes to a large plus symbol.
3   Drag to specify the width and height of the text box.
4   Type to enter text in the text box.

Alternatively, you can insert a built-in text box by clicking Text Box and selecting one of the options from the gallery.

You can resize a text box by dragging any of its sizing handles. When you create or work with text boxes, Word displays the Drawing Tools | Format tab on the Ribbon.

You can format text boxes in a number of ways. For example, you can click Text Direction, in the Text group on the Format tab, to specify that text flows vertically rather than horizontally. You can also apply effects by clicking the Shape Effects button in the Shape Styles group. For example, you can click Shape Effects and point to Shadow to see options for adding shadows to a text box.

Linking text boxes

If you have two or more text boxes, you can link them to allow text to flow continuously from one text box to the next. To link two text boxes:

1   Enter the text in one text box, and keep that text box selected.
2   On the Drawing Tools | Format tab, in the Text group, click Create Link.
3   Click the empty text box where you want the text to be continued.

To break a link between text boxes, select any of the linked text boxes; then, in the Text group on the Format tab, click Break Link. The link will be broken for each text box linked after the selected text box.

Do it!   **B-3: Inserting a text box**

Here's how	Here's why
1 Click a blank area of the document	To deselect the shape you've drawn.
2 Click the **Insert** tab	
In the Text group, click **Text Box**	To display the Text Box gallery.
Select **Simple Text Box**	To create a basic text box with some placeholder text.
3 Type **Four regional directors will be appointed in the next fiscal year**	
4 Position and resize the text box as shown	Drag the text box to move it, and use the resize handles to resize it.
5 Update the document	

Formatting text boxes

Explanation

You can format a text box, and you can format the text within a text box. To select and format the text in a text box, use the same techniques you'd use to select and format text in a typical document.

When you select a text box, the Drawing Tools | Format tab appears. Use the groups on this tab to format the text box itself.

Do it!

B-4:   Formatting a text box

The files for this activity are in Student Data folder **Unit 6\Topic B**.

Here's how	Here's why
1 Click inside the text box	To place the insertion point in it.
Press `CTRL` + `A`	
Format the text as Trebuchet MS, 9 pt, right-aligned	Use the Font group on the Home tab.
2 Resize the text box until it is just large enough to display all of the text as shown	
	(Drag the sizing handles.) Next, you'll change the text box's fill and outline.
3 With the text box selected, click the **Format** tab	Under Drawing Tools.
4 In the Shape Styles group, click the **Shape Outline** arrow and choose **No Outline**	To remove the visible border from the text box.
5 In the Shape Styles group, click the More button, as shown	
	To display the gallery.
Select the indicated option	
	Moderate Effect - Orange, Accent 6.
6 Update the document	

Arranging objects

Explanation

When you create multiple text boxes or shapes, you might need to change how they overlap one another or align with one another. You can arrange text boxes and shapes by using the tools on the Drawing Tools | Format tab. The Arrange group contains options for specifying how objects overlap and align with one another.

Stacking order

The order in which objects overlap is known as the *stacking order*. Newer shapes or text boxes you create will appear in front of older items if they overlap. To change the stacking order, select an item and then select an option from the Arrange group on the Drawing Tools | Format tab. You can click the Bring Forward or Send Backward buttons, or you can click either button's arrow to display a menu with additional options for adjusting the stacking order.

Alignment

To align shapes or text boxes with one another:

1   Select the items you want to align.
2   Click the Drawing Tools | Format tab.
3   In the Arrange group, click Position and choose the type of alignment you want.

Do it!

B-5:   Arranging multiple objects

Here's how	Here's why
1 Select the text box	(If necessary.) Click the edge of the text box.
2 Press → several times	
	To nudge the text box to the right so that it overlaps the arrow's left edge. When the text box and arrow shape overlap, the text box appears on top because it was created more recently. You'll send the text box to the back so that the arrow shape appears in front of it.
3 In the Arrange group, click the arrow next to Send Backward and choose **Send to Back**	To send the text box to the back of the stacking order.
4 Nudge the text box	
	So that the arrow doesn't overlap the text.
5 Update the document	

Changing shapes into different shapes

Explanation

After creating a shape or text box, you can convert it to a different shape. For example, after you create an arrow shape and apply formatting to it, you might decide to change to a different type of arrow (or a different shape altogether). If you delete the current shape and start over, you'll have to draw the new shape and reapply all the formatting you applied to the old shape. However, if you simply change the current shape, it will appear as the new shape but will retain any formatting you've already applied.

To change one shape into another:

1 Select the shape.
2 Click the Drawing Tools | Format tab.
3 In the Insert Shapes group, click the Edit Shape button and point to Change Shape.
4 Select the desired shape.

Do it!

B-6: Changing a shape into another shape

Here's how	Here's why
1 Select the text box	If necessary.
2 Click the **Format** tab	(Under Drawing Tools, if necessary.) You'll change the text box shape.
3 In the Insert Shapes group, click [icon]	The Edit Shape button.
Point to **Change Shape**	To display the Shapes gallery.
Under Flowchart, select the indicated shape	(Flowchart: Alternate Process.) To change the text box to a rounded rectangle.
4 Nudge the text box	If necessary, to arrange it relative to the arrow.
5 Update and close the document	

Topic C: Formatting text graphically

This topic covers the following Microsoft Office Specialist objectives for exam 77-881: Word 2010.

#	Objective
3.3	**Construct content in a document by using the Quick Parts tool**
	3.3.1 Add built-in building blocks
	3.3.1.1 Quotes
4.2	**Insert and format shapes, WordArt, and SmartArt**
	4.2.4 Set shape styles
	4.2.4.2 Text

Graphical text effects

Explanation

Word provides various ways you can apply graphical effects to text to add visual interest to a document. You can create WordArt objects, use drop caps, and add pull quotes.

Working with WordArt

The "flag" of a newsletter (i.e., the newsletter's name) and the headline of a flyer are often stylized, as are other document elements that you might want to draw attention to. One way to stylize text is to use WordArt to create decorative effects from text. You can create WordArt from existing text or insert a new text box.

To create WordArt from existing text in a document, first select the text. Then, in the Text group on the Insert tab, click WordArt and select a style from the gallery, shown in Exhibit 6-6. (If no text is selected, Word creates the WordArt object with the placeholder "Your text here.") You can format the text as you would regular text in the document.

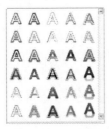

Exhibit 6-6: The WordArt gallery

When you select WordArt that has been inserted in a document, the Drawing Tools | Format tab appears on the Ribbon. Using the tools on this tab, you can further modify the decorative text. You can change the spacing of the text, change the WordArt style, add or modify shadow effects, modify 3-D effects, and change the position of the text in the document, among other things.

Do it!

C-1: Using WordArt

The files for this activity are in Student Data folder **Unit 6\Topic C**.

Here's how	Here's why
1 Open Announcement	
Save the document as **My announcement**	In the current topic folder.
2 Select the first line of text	"A word from the chairman."
3 Click the **Insert** tab	
In the Text group, click **WordArt**	To open the WordArt gallery.
Select the indicated WordArt style	(Gradient Fill - Blue, Accent 1.) To create WordArt from the selection. Word automatically creates a text box for the WordArt.
4 In the WordArt Styles group, click [A ·]	The Text Effects button.
Point to **Reflection**	
Select the indicated option	Reflection Variations Tight Reflection, touching.
5 Update the document	

Using drop caps

Explanation

A *drop cap* is a large initial capital letter that extends below the first line of text in a paragraph. The drop cap adds visual interest and can be used to begin a document or a chapter, for example.

There are two variations of a drop cap: *dropped* and *in-margin*. Exhibit 6-7 shows a dropped drop cap; notice the way the text wraps around and below the dropped letter. Exhibit 6-8 shows an in-margin drop cap.

> We're delighted to present this edition of Outlander Cooking!, revised and expanded for 2010.
>
> Inside, you'll find just enough information about our spices to whet your appetite. You'll also find some of our favorite recipes, compiled by our staff in response to your letters and emails, telling us about how you've been using our spices.

Exhibit 6-7: A dropped drop cap

> We're delighted to present this edition of Outlander Cooking!, revised and expanded for 2010.
>
> Inside, you'll find just enough information about our spices to whet your appetite. You'll also find some of our favorite recipes, compiled by our staff in response to your letters and emails, telling us about how you've been using our spices.

Exhibit 6-8: An in-margin drop cap

To add a drop cap, place the insertion point in the paragraph that you want to begin with a drop cap. On the Insert tab, click Drop Cap in the Text group and select the type of drop cap you want.

You can change the font of the drop-cap letter and change the distance of the text around it. To make such modifications, select the drop cap, click Drop Cap on the Insert tab, and choose Drop Cap Options to open the Drop Cap dialog box.

Do it!   **C-2:   Inserting and modifying a drop cap**

Here's how	Here's why
1 Place the insertion point in the first paragraph	It begins with "We're delighted to present."
2 Click the **Insert** tab	
3 In the Text group, click **Drop Cap**	
Point to **In margin**	To see a preview in the document.
Select **Dropped**	To create a drop cap.
4 In the Text group, click **Drop Cap**	
Choose **Drop Cap Options...**	To open the Drop Cap dialog box.
Observe the options	In addition to changing the position of the drop cap or removing it altogether, you can change its font and its distance from the text around it.
5 From the Font list, select **Brush Script MT**	To assign a different font to the drop cap.
Edit the "Lines to drop" box to read **5**	To increase the size of the capital letter to span five lines.
6 Click **OK**	To apply the changes.
7 Update the document	

Adding pull quotes to a document

Explanation   A *pull quote* is a brief phrase excerpted from body text. (It doesn't have to be an actual quotation.) This phrase or quote is typically enlarged or set apart from the body text by other formatting, as shown in Exhibit 6-9. You can use pull quotes to emphasize specific phrases or quotes and to add visual interest to a document.

To insert pull quotes in a document:

1 On the Insert tab, in the Text group, click Text Box.

2 In the Text Box gallery, select the style of pull quote you want to use.

3 In the text box, enter the desired phrase or quote.

4 Using the Drawing Tools | Format tab, you can change the appearance of the text box as desired.

5 Drag and resize the text box as needed.

W e're delighted to present this edition of Outlander Cooking!, revised and expanded for 2010.

Inside, you'll find just enough information about our spices to whet your appetite. You'll also find some of our favorite recipes, compiled by our staff in response to your letters and emails, telling us about how you've been using our spices.

Also, be sure to check out our Web site, outlanderspices.com, for even more recipes, as well as for ordering information. All the spices used in this book are available for immediate ordering, and we stock many more. If you don't see it, ask, and we'll track it down for you.

We're sure you'll find enough here to keep you cooking for some time!

Exhibit 6-9: A pull quote

Do it!

C-3:   Inserting a pull quote

Here's how	Here's why
1 Select the fourth body paragraph	It begins "We're sure you'll find enough here." You'll place this text in a pull quote.
2 Press (CTRL) + (C)	To copy the text from the document and place it on the Clipboard.
3 On the Insert tab, in the Text group, click **Text Box**	To open the gallery.
Select **Austere Quote**	To insert a text box with that style.
4 Press (CTRL) + (V)	To paste the text you copied earlier.
Press (CTRL)	To show the Paste Options.
Press (T)	To select the Keep Text Only option.
5 Drag the text box to the location shown	The document text automatically wraps around the text box.

W e're delighted to present this edition of Outlander Cooking!, revised and expanded for 2010.

Inside, you'll find just enough information about our spices to whet your appetite. You'll also find some of our favorite recipes, compiled by our staff in response to your letters and emails, telling us about how you've been using our spices.

Also, be sure to check out our Web site, outlanderspices.com, for even more recipes, as well as for ordering information. All the spices used in this book are available for immediate ordering, and we stock many more. If you don't see it, ask, and we'll track it down for you.

We're sure you'll find enough here to keep you cooking for some time!

6 Update and close the document

Unit summary: Graphics

Topic A   In this topic, you used the **SmartArt** feature to create an organization chart, and you used the SmartArt Tools to modify the organization chart.

Topic B   In this topic, you created and modified a **shape**. You also inserted and formatted a **text box**. In addition, you learned how to arrange multiple objects by changing their **alignment** and **stacking order**. Finally, you converted a shape into a different shape.

Topic C   In this topic, you used **WordArt** and **drop caps** to format text graphically. You also inserted a **pull quote** in a document. You learned that by making dramatic visual changes to text, you can add interest and visual appeal to a document.

Independent practice activity

In this activity, you'll create and format a process chart. You'll also insert and format a text box.

1 Create a new, blank document. Save it as **My practice graphics** in Student Data folder Unit 6\Unit summary.

2 Create a process chart that uses the Basic Process SmartArt graphic.

3 Name the diagram boxes **Meet new supplier**, **Examine products**, and **Finalize approval**.

4 Add a fourth box with the text **Follow up**, as shown in Exhibit 6-10. (*Hint:* In the Text pane, with the last text item selected, press Enter.)

5 Apply the Colorful Range - Accent Colors 3 to 4 color scheme. (*Hint:* Click the Change Colors button on the SmartArt Tools | Design tab.)

6 Change the "Follow up" box to Orange, Accent 6, Darker 25%. (*Hint:* Use the SmartArt Tools | Format tab.)

7 Draw a text box above the "Examine products" box. (*Hint:* Use the Insert tab.)

8 In the text box, enter **Test all products we plan to purchase**.

9 Format the text as Trebuchet MS, 10 pt, centered.

10 Change the text box shape to the Down Arrow Callout shape, as shown in Exhibit 6-11. (*Hint:* Use the Drawing Tools | Format tab.)

11 Resize and reposition the text box as shown in Exhibit 6-12.

12 Fill the text box with the color of your choice.

13 Update and close the document.

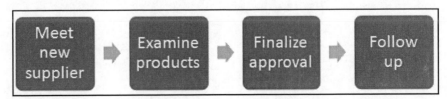

Exhibit 6-10: The process chart at the end of Step 4

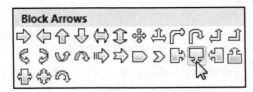

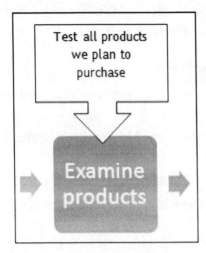

Exhibit 6-11: Selecting the new shape described in Step 10

Exhibit 6-12: The final text box shape as it appears after Step 11

Review questions

1 Which button on the Insert tab should you use to create a diagram?

   A Picture

   B SmartArt

   C Chart

   D Clip Art

2 How can you add text within a SmartArt diagram?

   A Draw a text box over the diagram box.

   B On the Insert tab, click Insert Object and choose Object.

   C Right-click the box and choose Insert Text.

   D Enter text in the Text pane.

3 Which Ribbon tab should you use to change the color of a single box in a diagram?

   A SmartArt Tools | Format

   B SmartArt Tools | Design

   C Home

   D Page Layout

4 How can you create a shape that contains text? (Choose all that apply.)

   A On the Insert tab, click Text Box and choose Draw Text Box.

   B Draw a shape, click the Drawing Tools | Format tab, and click Text Wrapping.

   C Draw a shape, right-click it, and choose Add Text.

   D Draw a shape, click the Drawing Tools | Format tab, and click Shape Fill.

5 If a selected shape appears on top of another shape, where they overlap, how can you move the selected shape behind the other shape?

   A On the Drawing Tools | Format tab, click Change Shape.

   B On the Drawing Tools | Format tab, click Send Backward.

   C On the Drawing Tools | Format tab, click Align and choose Align Top.

   D On the Drawing Tools | Format tab, click Align and choose Align Bottom.

6 Where are the WordArt and Drop Cap tools located?

   A In the WordArt Styles group on the SmartArt Tools | Format tab

   B In the Design group on the Page Layout tab

   C In the Text group on the Insert tab

   D In the Styles group on the WordArt Tools | Format tab

Unit 7

Managing document revisions

Unit time: 45 minutes

Complete this unit, and you'll know how to:

A Track changes while editing, review and accept revisions, view changes made by different reviewers, restrict edits to tracked changes, and merge revisions.

B Insert, print, and delete comments.

Topic A: Tracking changes

This topic covers the following Microsoft Office Specialist objectives for exam 77-881: Word 2010.

#	Objective
1.1	**Share and maintain documents**
	1.1.3 Arrange windows
	1.1.3.1 View Side by Side
	1.1.3.2 Synchronous Scrolling
	1.1.4 Arrange document views
	1.1.4.5 Draft
5.3	**Insert and modify comments in a document**
	5.3.4 View a comment
	5.3.4.1 View comments from another user
	5.3.4.2 View comments inline
	5.3.4.3 View comments as balloons

This topic covers the following Microsoft Office Specialist objectives for exam 77-887: Word Expert 2010.

#	Objective
1.1	**Configure Word options**
	1.1.1 Change default program options
1.2	**Apply protection to a document**
	1.2.1 Restrict editing
3.1	**Review, compare, and combine documents**
	3.1.1 Apply tracking
	3.1.2 Merge different versions of a document
	3.1.3 Track changes in a combined document

Managing revisions

Explanation

Your document might need to be reviewed by colleagues before it's finalized. If so, you can maintain a record of who makes which changes, and then you can choose to accept or reject each change. You can use the Track Changes feature to view changes and comments, and you can see changes made by specific reviewers. A *reviewer* is a person who evaluates a document and changes it.

Using Track Changes

To use the Track Changes feature, you must first turn it on. To do so, either click the Review tab and click the Track Changes button in the Tracking group, or press Ctrl+Shift+E. Changes that you or another reviewer make will appear in different colors and can appear with different formatting. For example, you can choose to have deletions appear in red with bold formatting.

To modify the settings for Track Changes, click the Review tab. Click Track Changes and choose Change Tracking Options to open the Track Changes Options dialog box, shown in Exhibit 7-1. Then specify the settings you want to use to indicate changes.

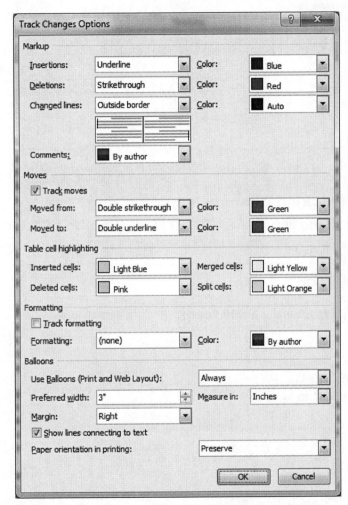

Exhibit 7-1: The Track Changes Options dialog box

When the document is in Draft or Outline view, markups appear inline with the text. However, you can also view markups in Print Layout, Full Screen Reading, and Web Layout views. In these views, some markups appear in balloons (similar to callouts) in the margin, as shown in Exhibit 7-2. To control the location and appearance of the balloons, use the Balloons section of the Track Changes Options dialog box.

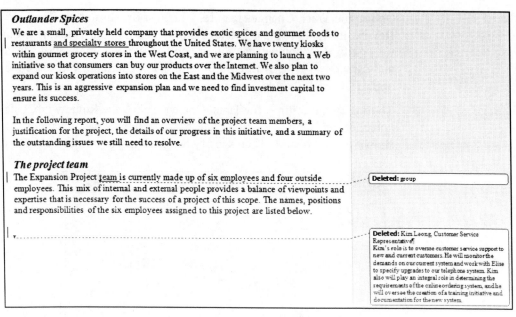

Outlander Spices

We are a small, privately held company that provides exotic spices and gourmet foods to restaurants and specialty stores throughout the United States. We have twenty kiosks within gourmet grocery stores in the West Coast, and we are planning to launch a Web initiative so that consumers can buy our products over the Internet. We also plan to expand our kiosk operations into stores on the East and the Midwest over the next two years. This is an aggressive expansion plan and we need to find investment capital to ensure its success.

In the following report, you will find an overview of the project team members, a justification for the project, the details of our progress in this initiative, and a summary of the outstanding issues we still need to resolve.

The project team

The Expansion Project team is currently made up of six employees and four outside employees. This mix of internal and external people provides a balance of viewpoints and expertise that is necessary for the success of a project of this scope. The names, positions and responsibilities of the six employees assigned to this project are listed below.

Deleted: group

Deleted: Kim Leong, Customer Service Representative¶
Kim's role is to oversee customer service support to new and current customers. He will monitor the demands on our current system and work with Elise to specify upgrades to our telephone system. Kim also will play an integral role in determining the requirements of the online ordering system, and he will oversee the creation of a training initiative and documentation for the new system.

Exhibit 7-2: Tracked changes and corresponding balloons in Print Layout view

Do it!

A-1: Tracking changes while editing

The files for this activity are in Student Data folder **Unit 7\Topic A**.

Here's how	Here's why
1 Open Team	
Save the document as **My team**	In the current topic folder.
2 Click the **Review** tab	
In the Tracking group, click **Track Changes**, as shown	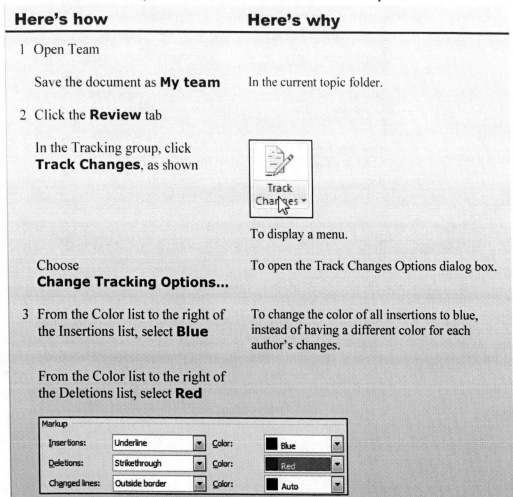 To display a menu.
Choose **Change Tracking Options...**	To open the Track Changes Options dialog box.
3 From the Color list to the right of the Insertions list, select **Blue**	To change the color of all insertions to blue, instead of having a different color for each author's changes.
From the Color list to the right of the Deletions list, select **Red**	

4 From the Use Balloons (Print and Web Layout) list, select **Always**

   Click **OK**   To close the Track Changes Options dialog box.

5 In the Tracking group, click the top half of the Track Changes button

   To enable change tracking. (If this feature is enabled, clicking the button again will disable it.)

6 Under "Outlander Spices," insert **and specialty stores**, as shown

   Outlander Spices

   We are a small, privately held company tha
   restaurants and specialty stores throughout

7 Under "The project team," select **group**

   The project team
   The Expansion Project group is currently
   employees. This mix of internal and exter

   Type **team**   The inserted text is blue and underlined, while the deleted text appears in a red balloon in the margin. A vertical line in the left margin indicates a change.

8 At the end of the document, delete the text about Kim Leong, as shown

   teas are in high demand in each of the regions into which we plan to expand. Ron also will monitor the data on Web purchases and buying trends in the new markets. In addition, he will work with our vendors to ensure that the supply of teas and spices supports the increased sales we expect from this initiative.

   Deleted: Kim Leong, Customer Service Representative¶
   Kim's role is to oversee customer service support to new and current customers. He will monitor the demands on our current system and work with Elise to specify upgrades to our telephone system. Kim also will play an integral role in determining the requirements of the online ordering system, and he will oversee the creation of a training initiative and documentation for the new system.

9 On the View tab, click **Draft**   To switch to Draft view. The markup appears inline, rather than in the margin.

   Switch back to Print Layout view

10 Update the document

Reviewing revisions

Explanation

When someone else edits your work and returns it for your approval, you'll probably want to review the suggested changes. As you review the changes, you can either accept or reject them.

To accept or reject a change, select it and click either Accept or Reject on the Review tab. You can accept or reject all of the changes at once by clicking Accept and choosing Accept All Changes in Document or by clicking Reject and choosing Reject All Changes in Document. To quickly find changes in a document, click Next or Previous in the Changes group on the Review tab.

Do it!   **A-2:   Reviewing and accepting revisions**

Here's how	Here's why
1 Place the insertion point at the beginning of the document	(Press Ctrl+Home.) You'll review the revisions.
2 On the Review tab, in the Changes group, click **Next**	To select the first change in the document—you inserted "and specialty stores."
In the Changes group, click the Accept button	To accept this change and move to the next one.
3 Click the Accept button twice	To accept the deletion and insertion. Because you replaced text, there are actually two changes to review—the deletion of the original text, and the insertion of the new text—before moving on to the next change.
4 Click the Reject button	To reject the deletion of the text about Kim Leong. A message box states that there are no more comments or tracked changes in the document.
Click **OK**	To accept the message.
5 Verify that the text from "Kim Leong" to the end of the document is selected	
Drag the selection to the left of "Aileen MacElvoy," as shown	Aileen MacElvoy. Director of Marketing Aileen's role is to oversee market research the Sales force. She will also oversee all m vendors, as well as act as the project spoke parties.
	To move the selected text. It appears in green to indicate that it was moved.
6 Press →	To place the insertion point after the text you moved.
Press ↵ ENTER twice	To separate the two paragraphs.
7 Update and close the document	

Multiple reviewers

Explanation

You might want to view only the revisions or only the comments inserted in a document. On the Review tab, in the Tracking group, click Show Markup and choose which elements to show or hide. For example, to view only the comments, click the other options to deselect them—by default, all of the options are selected.

You can also choose to view only the changes made by specific people. Click Show Markup and choose Reviewers to display a list with each reviewer's name, as shown in Exhibit 7-3. By default, All Reviewers is checked. To see only the changes made by a specific person, first deselect all reviewers by choosing All Reviewers; then select the reviewer or reviewers whose revisions or comments you want to see.

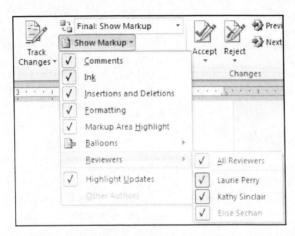

Exhibit 7-3: A list of reviewers for a document

Personalizing Word

To be identified by name as a reviewer, as shown in Exhibit 7-3, personalize your copy of Word. On the Review tab, in the Tracking group, click Track Changes and choose Change User Name to open the Word Options dialog box. Under "Personalize your copy of Microsoft Office," type your name in the User name box.

Do it! **A-3: Viewing changes by different reviewers**

The files for this activity are in Student Data folder **Unit 7\Topic A**.

Here's how	Here's why
1 Open Review1	
Save the document as **My review1**	In the current topic folder.
2 Scroll in the document	To see the changes made by all of the reviewers.
3 Click the **Review** tab	
In the Tracking group, click **Show Markup** and choose **Reviewers, All Reviewers**	To clear the All Reviewers option, turning it off.
4 Click **Show Markup** and choose **Reviewers, Elise Sechan**	To show only markups added by Elise Sechan.
Scroll in the document	To see the changes made by Elise Sechan.
5 Click **Show Markup** and choose **Reviewers, Kathy Sinclair**	To see both Elise Sechan's and Kathy Sinclair's changes.
	You'll add yourself as a reviewer.
6 Click **Track Changes** and choose **Change User Name...**	To open the Word Options dialog box.
In the User name box, type your name	
In the Initials box, type your initials	
Click **OK**	
7 Enable Track Changes	Click the Track Changes button or press Ctrl+Shift+E.
8 Under "Outlander Spices," edit the indicated text to read **online**	*Outlander Spices*¶ We·are·a·small,·privately·held·company·tha restaurants·throughout·the·United·States.·W stores·in·the·West·Coast,·and·we·are·plannir can·buy·our·products over·the·Internet.·We· stores·on·the·East·and·in·the·Midwest·over·t
9 Click **Show Markup** and choose **Reviewers, All Reviewers**	Your name now appears in the list of document reviewers.
10 Update the document	

Restricting edits

Explanation

If you want to protect a document from unwanted edits, you can restrict the edits to only tracked changes. In other words, any changes that someone makes will automatically be recorded as tracked changes. Then when the document is returned, you can decide whether to accept or reject the changes.

To restrict editing to tracked changes:

1 On the Review tab, in the Protect group, click Restrict Editing to open the Restrict Formatting and Editing pane.

2 Under Editing restrictions, check "Allow only this type of editing in the document."

3 From the list under Editing restrictions, select Tracked changes.

4 Under Start enforcement, click Yes, Start Enforcing Protection.

5 In the "Enter new password (optional)" box, enter a password.

6 In the "Reenter password to confirm" box, enter the same password.

7 Click OK.

If you want to accept or reject the changes in a protected document, you first need to unprotect it.

Do it!

A-4: Restricting edits to tracked changes

Here's how	Here's why
1 On the Review tab, in the Protect group, click **Restrict Editing**	To open the Restrict Formatting and Editing pane.
2 Under Editing restrictions, check **Allow only this type of editing in the document**	
From the list under Editing restrictions, select **Tracked changes**	To prevent other users from making untracked changes and from accepting or rejecting tracked changes. You'll be the only person who can accept or reject the changes in this document.
3 Under Start enforcement, click **Yes, Start Enforcing Protection**	
In the "Enter new password (optional)" box, type **password**	Anyone who knows this password will be able to accept or reject the tracked changes.
In the "Reenter password to confirm" box, type **password**	
Click **OK**	To apply the password settings. The Restrict Formatting and Editing pane displays a message stating that the document is password-protected and all edits will be tracked.

4 Under "The project team," change "outside employees" to **external consultants**	In the first sentence of the first paragraph under the heading "The project team."
5 Select **external**	(The word you just added.) The Accept and Reject buttons are disabled. You're not allowed to accept or reject changes made in the document.
6 In the Restrict Formatting and Editing pane, click **Stop Protection** In the Password box, type **password** Click **OK**	 The Accept and Reject buttons on the Ribbon are enabled again.
7 In the Changes group, click the arrow under Accept and choose **Accept All Changes in Document**	
8 Close the Restrict Formatting and Editing pane	
9 Update the document	

Working with multiple documents at once

Explanation

If you want to work on multiple documents simultaneously, it's helpful to view them simultaneously. To do so, first open all the documents you want to work with. Then, on the View tab, in the Window group, click Arrange All.

If you have two documents open simultaneously, you can view them side by side. On the View tab, in the Window group, click View Side by Side. By default, the windows will scroll synchronously to help you compare their content.

Do it!

A-5:   Managing multiple documents simultaneously

The files for this activity are in Student Data folder **Unit 7\Topic A**.

Here's how	Here's why
1 Open Review2	This was originally the same document as the document you have open, but it has been edited.
2 Click the **View** tab	
In the Window group, click **View Side by Side**	To display both documents simultaneously.
In the Window group, observe the Synchronous Scrolling button	This option is selected by default.
Press (ESC)	To close the Window group.
3 Scroll through either document	(Use both the horizontal and vertical scrollbars.) As you scroll in one document, the other document scrolls synchronously.
4 Close Review2	
Close My review1	

Merging revisions into a new document

Explanation

There might be times when several copies of the same document have been circulating for reviewers to mark up. Trying to manually combine all of the reviewers' marks into one document would be tedious. Instead, you can review the changes from two documents, decide which to keep, and then merge the two documents into a single document.

To merge two copies of a document in which changes have been tracked:

1 Click the Review tab.

2 In the Compare group, click Compare and choose Combine to open the Combine Documents dialog box.

3 From the Original document list, select the first marked-up document.

4 From the Revised document list, select the second marked-up document.

5 Click More to display additional options in the dialog box.

6 Under Comparison settings, check all items that you want Word to compare.

7 Under "Show changes in," select either Original document or Revised document (to identify which document the combined results should be shown in).

8 Click OK.

All tracked changes appear as marked revisions in the merged document, which appears in the Combined Document pane, as shown in Exhibit 7-4. The two original documents appear in the Original Document and Revised Document panes. In addition, a Summary pane provides a summary of all revisions in both documents. As in any other document, you can accept or reject each change.

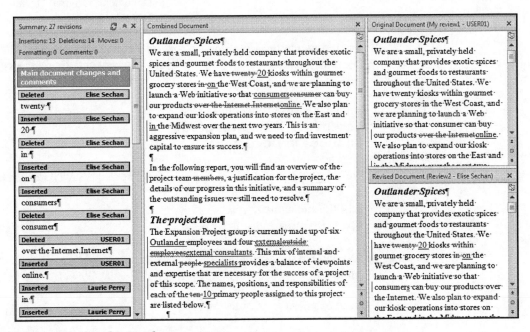

Exhibit 7-4: Combining documents

Do it!

A-6: Merging revisions

The files for this activity are in Student Data folder **Unit 7\Topic A**.

Here's how	Here's why
1 Click the **Review** tab	You'll merge two documents into one document that contains the changes from both.
In the Compare group, click **Compare**	
Choose **Combine...**	To open the Combine Documents dialog box.
2 From the Original document list, select **My review1**	
From the Revised document list, select **Review2**	These were originally the same document, but they now contain different changes.
3 Click **More**	To show more options for combining documents.
Under "Show changes in," select **New document**	If necessary.
Click **OK**	Several panes appear: Summary, Combined Document, Original Document, and Revised Document.
4 Scroll down in the Combined Document pane	To examine the changes. The Original Document and Revised Document panes scroll as well.
5 In the Changes group, click **Accept** and choose **Accept All Changes in Document**	
6 Press CTRL + S	To open the Save As dialog box.
Edit the file name to read **My combined document**	
Navigate to the current topic folder	If necessary.
Click **Save**	
7 Press CTRL + W	To close all open panes.

Topic B: Working with comments

This topic covers the following Microsoft Office Specialist objectives for exam 77-881: Word 2010.

#	Objective
5.3	**Insert and modify comments in a document**
	5.3.1 Insert a comment
	5.3.2 Edit a comment
	5.3.3 Delete a comment

This topic covers the following Microsoft Office Specialist objectives for exam 77-887: Word Expert 2010.

#	Objective
3.1	**Review, compare, and combine documents**
	3.1.4 Review comments in a combined document

Inserting comments

Explanation

While reviewing a document, you might want to insert suggestions or comments. In Print Layout view, comments appear in balloons in the margin, as shown in Exhibit 7-5. Each comment appears with the initials of the person who made it (assuming that the initials were entered in the General section of the Word Options dialog box).

To insert comments in a document:

1 Select the text that you want to comment on. This text will be highlighted after the comment is added.

2 On the Review tab, in the Comments group, click New Comment.

3 Type your comment.

To edit a comment you made, simply type in its comment balloon. You can also view and edit comments in the Reviewing pane. To open it, click Reviewing Pane in the Tracking group.

To delete a comment, first place the insertion point either in the comment balloon or in the text to which the comment was added. Then, in the Comments group, click Delete.

You can review the changes and comments in a document by clicking Reviewing Pane in the Tracking group on the Review tab.

Ann Salinski, VP Financial Services
Ann's role is to oversee the financials for this project. She acts as the gatekeeper for all expenditures and has the final say on any cost overruns for the project. Ann is one of the founders of Outlander Spices, and she performs this financial management role in addition to her other duties at the company.

Comment [ST1]: Consider removing the text about Ann's other duties at the company to streamline this document.

Exhibit 7-5: Comments in Print Layout view

Do it!

B-1:   Inserting and modifying comments

The files for this activity are in Student Data folder **Unit 7\Topic B**.

Here's how	Here's why
1 Open Comments	
Save the document as **My comments**	In the current topic folder.
2 In Ann Salinski's paragraph, select **Ann's role**	*Ann Salinski, VP Financial Services* Ann's role is to oversee the financials
3 On the Review tab, in the Comments group, click **New Comment**	A comment bubble appears to the right of the document.
Type **Consider removing the text about Ann's other duties at the company.**	
4 In the Tracking group, click **Reviewing Pane**	To show comments and markups in the Reviewing pane.
5 In the Reviewing pane, click before the period at the end of the comment	To place the insertion point after the word "company" in the comment.
Press (SPACEBAR)	
Type **to streamline this document**	To modify the comment. The modification is reflected in the balloon.
In the Tracking group, click **Reviewing Pane**	To hide the pane.
6 Update and close the document	

Unit summary: Managing document revisions

Topic A   In this topic, you learned how to enable Word's **Track Changes** feature and change its settings. You also learned how to review and accept revisions, view changes made by different reviewers, and restrict edits to tracked changes. Finally, you learned how to **merge revisions** from two documents into one.

Topic B   In this topic, you learned how to work with **comments**.

Independent practice activity

In this activity, you'll enable Track Changes to record the revisions you make in a document. Then you'll compare your revisions with those of another reviewer and combine them into one document.

The files for this activity are in Student Data folder **Unit 7\Unit summary**.

1 Open Revisions practice, and save the document as **My revisions practice**.

2 Enable Track Changes.

3 On page 2, edit the heading "Healing benefits of herbs" to read **Health benefits of herbs**.

4 Accept all changes in the document.

5 Add this comment to the last line of the document: **Add a topic on commonly used herbs and spices**.

6 Update and close the document.

7 Compare the revisions in the documents My revisions practice and Second reviewer.

8 Scroll in the Combined Document pane to see the revisions from each reviewer.

9 Accept all changes in the combined document.

10 Save the document as **My combined revisions** and close it.

Review questions

1 How do you turn on the Track Changes feature?

2 In Print Layout view, with Track Changes turned on, where do deletions appear?

3 You want to send your document out for review, and you want to ensure that all edits are recorded as tracked changes. What should you do?

4 A document with comments is open and shown in Draft view. How can you read the comments?

Unit 8

Web features

Unit time: 45 minutes

Complete this unit, and you'll know how to:

A Preview a document as a Web page and save a document as a Web page.

B Insert a hyperlink in a document, use hyperlinks to navigate, and link to another document.

Topic A: Web pages

This topic covers the following Microsoft Office Specialist objectives for exam 77-881: Word 2010.

#	Objective
1.1	**Apply different views to a document**
	1.1.4 Arrange document views
	1.1.4.4 Web layout
1.4	**Share documents**
	1.4.1 Send documents via e-mail
	1.4.2 Send documents via SkyDrive
	1.4.3 Send documents via Internet fax
	1.4.4 Change file types
	1.4.6 Create
	1.4.7 Publish a blog post
	1.4.8 Register a blog account

Working with Web pages

Explanation

Web pages are built using *Hypertext Markup Language,* or *HTML,* which is a standard markup language that allows you to display text, images, and multimedia files on the Web. Even if you're not familiar with HTML, you can create a Web page in Word by saving a document as a Web page. You can also use Word to open and edit Web pages, and you can send Word documents through e-mail.

Web Layout view

While creating a Web page in Word, you might want to see how the document will look when viewed online. To do this, you can use Web Layout view.

To switch to Web Layout view, do either of the following:

- On the View tab, in the Document Views group, click Web Layout.
- Click the Web Layout button on the right side of the status bar.

Sharing documents electronically

As you work in Word and other Office programs, you might want to send a document you've created to another person via e-mail. Depending on the e-mail program you're using, the e-mail features and options might vary.

To send a Word document via e-mail, first open the document you want to send. Then, on the File tab, click Save & Send and click Send Using E-mail. Under Send Using E-mail, select an option for sending the document. For example, if you're not sure whether your recipient has Word, you might send the document as a PDF file.

You can also store a document online via SkyDrive, which requires a Windows Live ID. On the File tab, click Save & Send and then click Save to Web. Click Sign In and enter your Windows Live ID information. Then select a folder and click Save As to finish saving the document.

In addition, you can send documents via Internet fax. This requires the Windows Fax Printer Driver or Fax Services to be installed on your computer.

Do it!

A-1:   **Previewing a document as a Web page**

The files for this activity are in Student Data folder **Unit 8\Topic A**.

Here's how	Here's why
1 Open About us1	
2 Click the **View** tab	
In the Document Views group, click **Web Layout**	To display the document in Web Layout view. The document now appears as it would in a browser window.
3 Scroll through the document	Notice that there are no page breaks in Web Layout view, and the margins are optimized for online viewing.

Saving documents as Web pages

Explanation

You can save a Word document as a Web page. To do so, click the File tab and then click Save As. In the Save As dialog box, select Web Page from the Save as type list. The file will be saved as an HTML document with the extension .htm, and all of the graphics and images in the document will be saved in an associated folder. If you upload the Web page to a server, remember to include the folder containing the images for your page.

Changing the page title

The title bar of a Web page usually contains text called a *page title*, as shown in Exhibit 8-1. The title does not need to be long, but it should be descriptive.

To enter a new page title:

1 On the File tab, click Save As.
2 From the Save as type list, select Web Page.
3 Click Change Title.
4 Enter a descriptive title and click OK.
5 Click Save.

Exhibit 8-1: A title bar as displayed in a Web browser

Setting Web options

The Web Options dialog box, shown in Exhibit 8-2, contains a variety of settings you can use to tailor a document to your Web audience. For example, you can disable features that are not supported by certain browsers. To do so, click the Browsers tab and select a category of Web browsers. (Keep in mind that many people won't be using the latest versions.) Then check "Disable features not supported by these browsers" and click OK.

To open the Web Options dialog box:

1 On the File tab, click Save As.
2 From the Save as type list, select Web Page.
3 Click Tools and choose Web Options.

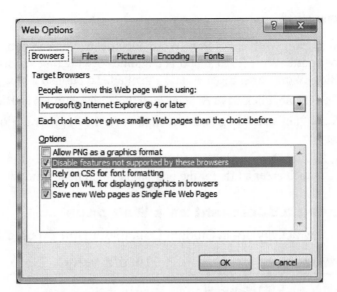

Exhibit 8-2: The Browsers tab in the Web Options dialog box

Opening HTML documents in a browser

A Web browser is software used to view Web sites, which contain Web pages. Several browser applications are available; one commonly used browser is Internet Explorer.

To open an HTML document in Internet Explorer:

1   Click the Start button and choose All Programs, Internet Explorer. (If your Windows desktop contains an Internet Explorer icon, you can double-click it.)

2   Choose File, Open; browse to and select the desired file; and click Open.

3   Click OK.

You can also open a file in a browser by typing or pasting the Web page's address into the browser's Address box and pressing Enter.

Opening HTML documents for editing in Word

You can edit an HTML document in Word. To do so, open the HTML file in Word, as you would open a Word document. Then modify the document as necessary, and save the file; it will automatically be resaved as an HTML document.

Blog posts

In addition to creating Web pages from Word documents, you can publish documents as *blog* (Web log) posts. Word 2010 supports a number of blogging services, such as SharePoint Blog, WordPress, Blogger, and TypePad. To publish a blog post:

1 On the File tab, click Save & Send, and then click Publish as Blog Post.

2 Click the Publish as Blog Post button to open the Register a Blog Account dialog box.

3 Click Register Now and follow the instructions to register your blog account. You can then enter a title for the post in the document window.

Do it!

A-2: Saving a document as a Web page

The files for this activity are in Student Data folder **Unit 8\Topic A**.

Here's how	Here's why
1 On the File tab, click **Save As**	
2 Navigate to the current topic folder	If necessary.
3 Edit the File name box to read **My web page**	
4 From the Save as type list, select **Web Page**	To save the document as a Web-page file with the .htm extension.
5 Click **Change Title**	
Edit the Page title box to read **About Outlander Spices**	The title will appear in the browser's title bar when this Web page is displayed.
Click **OK**	To close the dialog box. The title appears above the Change Title button.
6 Click **Save**	
7 Close the document	
8 In Windows Explorer, navigate to the current topic folder	
Observe the contents of the folder My web page_files	This folder contains image files and XML files used to display the HTML document. These files would need to accompany the Web page if you were to upload it to a server.

Topic B: Hyperlinks

This topic covers the following Microsoft Office Specialist objectives for exam 77-881: Word 2010.

#	Objective
6.1	**Apply a hyperlink**
	6.1.1 Apply a hyperlink to text or graphics
	6.1.3 Link a hyperlink to an e-mail address

Inserting hyperlinks

Explanation

A *hyperlink*, or *link* for short, is text or an image that, when clicked, connects to another page, another location on the same page, another site, or some other resource. When you point to a hyperlink in Word, a ScreenTip appears. By default, hyperlinks are blue and underlined; however, some Web pages contain formatting that changes the default appearance of hyperlinks.

In Word, you can use hyperlinks to link to a Web page, to another document, or to another place in the same document. You can also use hyperlinks to create a new document or send an e-mail message.

To insert a hyperlink in a document:

1   Select the text that you want to make a hyperlink.

2   On the Insert tab, in the Links group, click Hyperlink to open the Insert Hyperlink dialog box, shown in Exhibit 8-3. (You can also press Ctrl+K.)

3   To specify a ScreenTip for the hyperlink, click ScreenTip, enter the desired text, and click OK.

4   In the Address box, enter the location of the HTML file, Word document, or other file to which you want to link. To link to an e-mail address, click E-mail Address and enter the desired e-mail address.

5   Click OK.

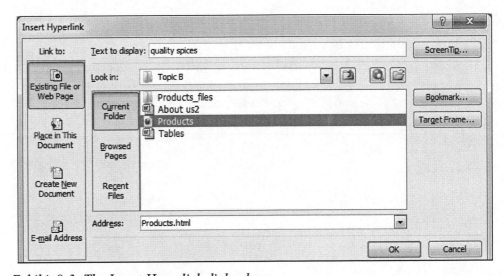

Exhibit 8-3: The Insert Hyperlink dialog box

Do it!

B-1:   Inserting a hyperlink to an HTML file

The files for this activity are in Student Data folder **Unit 8\Topic B**.

Here's how	Here's why
1 Open About us2	
Save the document as **My about us2**	In the current topic folder.
2 In the first paragraph, select **quality spices**	(In the second sentence.) You'll make this text a hyperlink.
Press (CTRL) + (K)	To open the Insert Hyperlink dialog box.
3 Click **ScreenTip**	To open the Set Hyperlink ScreenTip dialog box. You'll create a custom ScreenTip for your hyperlink to give users more information.
In the ScreenTip text box, type **Click to learn more about our products**	
Click **OK**	
4 Select **Products**	This is an HTML file containing product information.
5 Click **OK**	To create the hyperlink. The text "quality spices" is formatted to indicate that it's a hyperlink.
6 Update the document	

Using hyperlinks

Explanation

In a Web browser, you simply click a hyperlink to navigate to its associated content. To use a hyperlink in Word, however, you press and hold Ctrl, and then click the hyperlink. When you click a hyperlink, the mouse pointer must be in the shape of a pointing finger.

If a hyperlink points to a file, the linked file will open in its source program. After you click a link, its color typically changes to indicate that it has been clicked. This is known as a *followed hyperlink*.

Do it!

B-2:   Navigating with hyperlinks

Here's how	Here's why
1 Point to the hyperlink	Click to learn more about our products / Ctrl+Click to follow link / and l... spice / hest quality spices from all over the world and / etailers throughout the United States and Europ
	Word displays the ScreenTip you created, plus a message about how to follow the link.
2 Press and hold (CTRL)	Click to learn more about our products / Ctrl+Click to follow link / and ha... spice / hest quality spices from all over the world and / etailers throughout the United States and Europ
	The pointer changes to a pointing finger, indicating that this text is a hyperlink.
Click the hyperlink	To open the product information in your default browser.
3 Close your browser	To return to Word.
4 Observe the hyperlink	It has changed color, indicating that you've followed the link.

Linking to other types of files

Explanation

In addition to linking to Web pages, you can link to other types of files, such as Word or Excel files. For example, you might want to open a Word document that relates to some text in your current document, or you might want to open an Excel spreadsheet. To do this, you can create a hyperlink in the same way you would if you were linking to an HTML file.

Do it!

B-3:   Creating a hyperlink to a Word document

Here's how	Here's why
1 Under the "Expansion project" heading, select **kiosk operations**	You'll make this text a hyperlink to another Word document.
2 Press ⌨CTRL + ⌨K	
Select **Tables**	
Click **OK**	
3 Point to the hyperlink	
Observe the hyperlink's ScreenTip	The default ScreenTip displays the path of the linked file.
4 Press ⌨CTRL and click the hyperlink	To open the Tables document in Word.
5 Close the document	
6 Update and close My about us2	

Unit summary: Web features

Topic A   In this topic, you examined a document in Web Layout view. You also saved a document as a **Web page**.

Topic B   In this topic, you inserted a **hyperlink** to an HTML file, and you learned how to navigate by using hyperlinks. You also created a hyperlink that links to another Word document.

Independent practice activity

In this activity, you'll open a document and save it as a Web page. Then you'll insert a hyperlink that points to another HMTL file.

The files for this activity are in Student Data folder **Unit 8\Unit summary**.

1 Open Web practice, and save it as **My web practice**.

2 Preview the document as a Web page by using Web Layout view.

3 Save the file as a Web page named **My practice page**, and change the page title to **The Outlander Spices Team**.

4 In the first body paragraph, make the text **privately held company** a hyperlink to the file **About us**.

5 Use the hyperlink to display the HTML file.

6 Close your browser and return to Word.

7 Update and close the document.

8 Close Word. If prompted, do not save Building Blocks.

Review questions

1 How can you send a Word document as an e-mail attachment?

2 How can you check the appearance of your Web page before you save or publish it?

3 You want a title to appear in the browser's title bar when your Web page is opened. How do you edit a Web page's title in Word?

4 Describe the steps for inserting a hyperlink in a document.

Course summary

This summary contains information to help you bring the course to a successful conclusion. Using this information, you will be able to:

A Use the summary text to reinforce what you've learned in class.

B Determine the next courses in this series (if any), as well as any other resources that might help you continue to learn about Microsoft Word 2010.

Topic A: Course summary

Use the following summary text to reinforce what you've learned in class.

Unit summaries

Unit 1

In this unit, you learned how to examine text formatting and compare the formatting of two selections by using the **Reveal Formatting** pane. You also learned how to use and modify **styles**. You used styles to create an **outline**, and you learned how to organize and format an outline.

Unit 2

In this unit, you learned how to insert and delete **section breaks** and format sections. You also formatted text into **columns** and inserted column breaks.

Unit 3

In this unit, you learned how to align and orient **text in a table**. You also merged and split table cells, and you **resized rows**. Next, you changed a table's borders and applied shading to table cells. In addition, you used the Sort dialog box to **sort data** in a table. You then **split** a table, repeated a header row on multiple pages, and entered **formulas** in a table. Finally, you applied and modified **table styles**.

Unit 4

In this unit, you used the Envelopes and Labels dialog box to prepare and print a sheet of **address labels** and to print an address on a single **envelope**.

Unit 5

In this unit, you learned how to create a document from a **template**. Then you saved and used your own template. Next, you learned how to use the **Building Blocks Organizer**. In addition, you used the Restrict Formatting and Editing pane to **protect** a document with a password. Then you viewed and edited document **properties**. You also learned how to view a document's statistics.

Unit 6

In this unit, you used **SmartArt** to create and modify an organization chart. You also created and modified a **shape** and inserted and formatted a **text box**. In addition, you arranged objects by changing their alignment and stacking order. Next, you used WordArt and drop caps to **format text graphically**. Finally, you inserted a pull quote in a document.

Unit 7

In this unit, you learned how to enable Word's **Track Changes** feature and how to review and accept revisions, show changes made by different reviewers, and **restrict edits** to tracked changes. Then you learned how to **merge revisions** from two documents into one. You also learned how to work with **comments**.

Unit 8

In this unit, you examined a document in Web Layout view and saved a document as a **Web page**. You also inserted a **hyperlink** to an HTML file and learned how to use links to navigate. Finally, you created a hyperlink that links to another Word document.

Topic B: Continued learning after class

It is impossible to learn how to use any software effectively in a single day. To get the most out of this class, you should begin working with Microsoft Word 2010 to perform real tasks as soon as possible. We also offer resources for continued learning.

Next courses in this series

This is the second course in this series. The next course in this series is:

- *Word 2010: Advanced*
    - Set up a mail merge, and prepare labels and envelopes
    - Insert content from other applications, and work with document backgrounds
    - Create forms, and share and secure documents
    - Record, run, and modify macros
    - Customize the Quick Access toolbar and keyboard shortcuts
    - Use Word's features for working with long documents
    - Work with XML

Other resources

For more information, visit www.axzopress.com.

Glossary

Adjustment handle

A yellow diamond that appears if you can adjust a selected shape. You can drag an adjustment handle to reshape a drawn object.

Building block

A predefined portion of content—such as a cover page, header, or footer—that can be reused in a document.

Column break

A mark that indicates the end of a column.

Drawing canvas

A space where you can work on graphics or drawings in Word.

Drop cap

A large initial capital letter that extends below the first line of text in a paragraph.

Editing restrictions

A Word feature that enables you to protect a document by selecting the kind of editing allowed in it: Tracked Changes, Comments, Filling in forms, or No changes (Read only).

Field

A placeholder for data that can change, such as the current date and time.

Formatting restrictions

A Word feature that enables you to protect a document by preventing unauthorized users from modifying or using styles that you specify.

Formula

A mathematical statement used to perform arithmetic operations, such as calculating an average or a sum.

Function

A built-in formula used to perform calculations. For example, the SUM function adds the numbers in selected cells.

Header row

The first row in a table, typically containing descriptive headings for the data in each column.

Hyperlink

Text or an image that, when clicked, connects to another page, another location on the same page, another site, or some other resource.

Hypertext Markup Language (HTML)

A standard markup language that allows you to display text, images, and multimedia files on the Web.

Markups

In Word, the marks and colors that indicate insertions, deletions, formatting changes, and changed lines when Track Changes is used.

Metadata

Properties electronically associated with a document, such as the title and author.

Outline

A way of showing the structure of a document by displaying its headings and subheadings (if they're assigned an outline level).

Outline view

A Word view that enables you to collapse and expand text located under headings to see different levels of detail.

Page title

Text that describes a Web page and is displayed in the title bar of a browser.

Pull quote

A brief phrase excerpted from body text and placed in the document as a separate element.

Reviewer

A person who evaluates a document and changes it or comments on it.

Rotate handle

The green circle that appears near the top of a selected shape and is used to turn, or rotate, the shape.

Section

A portion of a document in which you can set certain formatting options—such as margins, headers and footers, page numbering, and page orientation—separately from the rest of the document.

Sidebar

A formatted text box that appears along the side of a document page.

Sizing handles

Circles that appear at each corner and along each edge of the boundary of a selected shape. You drag a sizing handle to resize the shape.

Stacking order
   The order in which objects in a document overlap one another.

Style
   A named set of formats, used to define the appearance of recurring text elements, such as headings or body text.

Template
   A document that contains formatting and boilerplate text or placeholder text and that is used to quickly create commonly used documents.

Text box
   A drawn object in which you can enter text. Text boxes can be placed anywhere in a document.

Thumbnails
   Miniature images of the pages in a document. Shown in the Navigation pane, thumbnails can be used to navigate through a document.

Index